TRUE CRIME CASE HISTORIES - VOLUME 21

12 DISTURBING TRUE CRIME STORIES

JASON NEAL

JASON NEAL BOOKS

Copyright © 2025 by Jason Neal.
True Crime Case Histories® is a registered trademark.
All rights reserved.

No part of this book may be reproduced in any form or by any electronic or mechanical means, including information storage and retrieval systems, without written permission from the author, except for the use of brief quotations in a book review.

Great effort and research have gone into the compilation of this material. It is the author's intention to represent the information within as accurately as possible. However, the author and publisher do not guarantee the accuracy of the text, graphics, and information presented. Any errors, omissions, or misinterpretations of this publication are not the responsibility of the author, copyright holder, or publisher. Although based on fact, some character names may have been changed, and/or scenes and dialogue may have been fictionalized. This publication is produced solely for informational and entertainment purposes and is not intended to hurt or defame anyone involved.

Cover images of:

Jesse Pratt: (top-left)

Leigh Ann Sabine: (top-right)

Anthony Pignitaro: (bottom-left)

Ariel Castro: (bottom-right)

More books by Jason Neal

Looking for more?? I am constantly adding new volumes of True Crime Case Histories. The series **can be read in any order**, and all books are available in paperback, hardcover, and audiobook.

Check out the complete series on Amazon series at:

https://geni.us/JasonNeal

As my way of saying "Thank you" for reading, I'm giving away a FREE True Crime e-book I think you'll enjoy.

https://TrueCrimeCaseHistories.com

Just visit the link above to let me know where to send your free book!

CONTENTS

Introduction	ix
1. The Salt Creek Monster	1
2. The Middletown Nightmare	19
3. The Body in the Garden	29
4. The Death Deal	45
5. The I-70 Rapist	57
6. The Perfect Murder	75
7. The Birthday Surprise	95
8. The Plastic Roses	117
9. The Bargain Basement	131
10. Imprint of Evil	145
11. They'll Blame Us	159
12. The Cleveland Monster	177
Online Appendix	195
Also by Jason Neal	197
Free Bonus Book	199
Thank You!	201
About the Author	203

INTRODUCTION

Evil leaves its mark.

Sometimes it's a tire track across a victim's body. Sometimes it's blood spatter in a closet that reveals years of hidden torture. Sometimes it's the careful placement of plastic roses beside a corpse—a killer's signature that makes no sense until you understand the twisted logic behind it.

The twelve cases in this book aren't random acts of violence or crimes of sudden passion. They're deliberate choices made by people who had plenty of time to reconsider, plenty of chances to stop, and plenty of warning signs they chose to ignore. These are stories of calculated cruelty that left permanent imprints on families, communities, and the investigators who had to piece together what happened.

What you're about to read includes graphic details that television true crime shows often sanitize or skip entirely. I include these details not to shock, but because understanding the full scope of these crimes requires confronting their reality without filters. The depths of human depravity can't be understood through euphemisms.

Each story has been meticulously researched using court transcripts, police reports, autopsy findings, and witness testimony. Some made headlines for weeks; others barely registered beyond their local communities, forgotten by everyone except the families still living with the aftermath. Many were suggested by readers who remembered these cases from their own hometowns or were personally affected by the events.

These aren't stories about criminal masterminds or Hollywood-style serial killers. They're about ordinary people who made the choice to destroy other ordinary people. A bus driver. A doctor. An aunt and uncle. The person next door who seemed perfectly normal—until the day they weren't.

A word of warning: This book contains descriptions of violence against children, sexual assault, and prolonged torture. If you're looking for redemption arcs or satisfying conclusions, you won't find them here. What you will find is the unvarnished truth about what humans are capable of when they decide that someone else's life is worth less than their own desires.

Some of these cases took decades to solve. Others were cracked within days. A few almost slipped through the cracks entirely, saved only by a mislabeled piece of evidence finally getting properly tested or a witness finally coming forward after years of silence.

For case photos and additional materials related to this volume, visit: TrueCrimeCaseHistories.com/vol21

Welcome to the dark corners of human nature that most people never have to see.

—Jason Neal

CHAPTER 1
THE SALT CREEK MONSTER

The afternoon sun cast long shadows across the sand dunes of Salt Creek when the fishermen first heard the screaming. It was February 2016, and Abdul-Karim Mohammed was checking his gear in the back of the moving SUV when a figure burst from the South Australian scrubland—a woman, naked and bloodied, running toward them with her arms flailing wildly above her head.

"He's going to kill us all!" she screamed in accented English, her voice raw with terror.

Abdul-Karim's father, Ali, slammed on the brakes as the woman threw herself into their moving vehicle, her body shaking violently. She was covered in scratches and bruises, sand stuck to the blood on her face. Abdul-Karim quickly grabbed a spare pair of pants and a jacket from their supplies, wrapping them around her as she trembled.

"My friend…" she gasped between sobs, gripping Abdul-Karim's arm with desperate strength. "Please, you have to find my friend. He has her. Please!"

The Mohammed family had come to this remote stretch of South Australian coastline for a peaceful fishing trip. The Coorong National Park, with its pristine beaches and untouched wilderness, stretched for miles in every direction. Salt Creek itself was barely a settlement—just twenty-nine residents and a roadhouse serving the occasional tourist brave enough to venture this far from civilization. There was no mobile phone coverage here, no quick way to call for help.

As more of their group arrived in two other SUVs, the woman's story tumbled out in fragments. Her name was Beatriz. She was Brazilian, twenty-three years old, and backpacking through Australia. There was another woman still out there—Lena, from Germany.

And there was a man. A man with a hammer.

The fishermen split up. Some drove Beatriz to the Salt Creek roadhouse while others turned back toward the dunes to search for Lena. Adam Stewart, the roadhouse owner, took one look at Beatriz's condition and immediately called the police. It would take officers two hours to reach this isolated location.

Back among the dunes, Ali Mohammed spotted something that made his blood run cold—a blood-soaked towel lying in the sand near an abandoned campsite. Nearby, a baseball cap, also drenched in blood. There was no sign of the German woman.

Then they saw her. Lena emerged from behind a sand dune, and for a moment, the men couldn't process what they were seeing. She was covered head to toe in blood—so much blood that they couldn't see the color of her skin beneath it.

Her blonde hair was matted into dark, wet clumps. She stumbled toward them, and one of the men noticed what looked like a tennis ball-sized lump protruding from her skull.

"Where is she?" Lena kept asking, her voice barely above a whisper. "Where is my friend? She saved my life."

Five days earlier, Beatriz had been sitting in a hostel in Adelaide, scrolling through Gumtree classified ads on her phone. She'd been in Australia for several months, working odd jobs and exploring the country on a shoestring budget. Now she wanted to get to Melbourne to meet up with some friends, but bus tickets were expensive. A rideshare would be cheaper.

She posted an ad: "Looking for a ride to Melbourne, happy to share petrol costs."

Several people responded, but most fell through—and then a message came from someone named Roman. He said he was driving to Melbourne and could take her. His messages were curt, almost impatient: "Just answer me. Tell me if you want to go with me or not."

Beatriz had learned to trust her instincts while traveling, and something about traveling alone with a stranger made her nervous. Thankfully, she'd already met Lena at the hostel—another twenty-three-year-old backpacker, this one from Germany, also heading in the same direction. They'd known each other for only a few days, but they got along well. When Beatriz mentioned the ride, Lena agreed to come along. Safety in numbers.

On February 9, 2016, they met Roman at Adelaide's Mawson Lakes railway station. The man who approached them was not what they'd expected. Roman Heinze stood six and a half feet tall, with a distinctive handlebar mustache and a balding head. At sixty years old, he was old enough to be their grandfather. His demeanor was gruff, his movements impatient. However, he had a large SUV with plenty of room for their backpacks, and he seemed to know the route well.

Roman Heinze

"I love the coast road," Roman told them as they loaded their bags. "Beautiful scenery. We can camp overnight at this place I know—Salt Creek. It's a great spot for seeing kangaroos."

The drive started normally enough. Roman talked about his life in Adelaide, how he used to be a chef but now took care of his elderly father. He seemed knowledgeable about the area, pointing out landmarks as they drove. But, as the hours passed and the landscape became more desolate, the conversation dried up. Roman's mood seemed to darken.

It was late afternoon when they turned off the main road and onto a sandy track. The path wound through scrubland and over dunes until finally, they emerged at a pristine beach. The ocean stretched endlessly before them, and there wasn't another soul in sight.

"This is Salt Creek," Roman announced, pulling to a stop among the dunes. "We'll camp here tonight."

Beatriz and Lena exchanged glances. This wasn't what they'd discussed. They thought they'd be staying at a campground with facilities and other people around, but Roman was already unloading camping gear from his vehicle.

———

As the sun began to set, painting the sand dunes in shades of gold and orange, Roman opened a bottle of wine. Lena, exhausted from the long drive, had crawled into the back of the SUV to take a nap. Beatriz sat with Roman near the campsite, accepting a glass of wine to be polite.

"Come on," Roman said suddenly, standing up. "Let's go look for kangaroos. They come out at dusk."

Beatriz looked back at the SUV where Lena was sleeping. Something felt off, but she couldn't put her finger on what. Roman was already walking away into the dunes, and she didn't want to seem rude, so she followed him.

They walked for several minutes, the campsite disappearing behind the rolling sand hills. The only sounds were the distant crash of the waves and the whisper of wind through the coastal grass. Roman stopped in a small hollow between two dunes.

"This is a good spot," he said, but his voice had changed. There was something different in his tone, something that made Beatriz's skin crawl.

She turned to head back to camp, but Roman grabbed her from behind. His large hands wrapped around her arms, and suddenly, she was being forced to the ground. She tried to scream, but he pushed her face into the sand. Something metal flashed in the dying light—a knife. He drove it into the sand beside her head.

"Don't move," he growled.

Beatriz's mind raced. This couldn't be happening. This was Australia, a safe country. She was supposed to be on her way to Melbourne to meet friends. Roman produced a rope from his pocket that he'd been carrying the entire time. He bound her wrists behind her back, then her ankles. The knife reappeared, and she felt the cold blade against her skin as he cut away her bikini.

"Please," she begged. "You don't need to do this."

But Roman wasn't listening. His hands were on her body, his mouth on her face and chest. She could smell the wine on his breath, feel his weight pressing her into the sand. When she tried to resist, he punched her in the face, the blow stunning her into temporary compliance.

Beatriz forced herself to think. She'd read stories of women who had survived attacks by staying calm, by thinking strategically. "We could go back to the camp," she said, trying to keep her voice steady. "It would be more comfortable there."

For a moment, Roman seemed to consider this. He pulled her to her feet, but instead of heading back toward camp, he started dragging her in the opposite direction, deeper into the dunes. That's when Beatriz knew with absolute certainty that he was going to kill her. She wasn't going to die here—not like this, not today.

She screamed with every ounce of strength in her body, a piercing shriek that cut through the evening air like a blade.

―――

Lena woke with a start. For a moment, she was disoriented—where was she? Then she remembered: the SUV, the trip to Melbourne, Salt Creek. But something was wrong. She could hear screaming in the distance. It was Beatriz.

She scrambled out of the vehicle and looked around. The campsite was empty. The screaming came again, from somewhere beyond the dunes. Lena ran toward the sound, her feet sinking into the soft sand with each step.

When she crested the dune, the scene before her seemed impossible. Beatriz was lying naked in the sand, her hands and feet bound with rope. Roman stood over her, and when he looked up at Lena, his expression was something she'd never forget.

"Let her go!" Lena shouted.

Roman's response was bizarre, almost casual: "I just wanted to try her."

He started walking toward Lena. Every instinct told her to run. She turned and sprinted back toward the SUV, thinking she could grab her phone and call for help. However, Roman was faster than his age suggested. She heard his footsteps pounding behind her, getting closer.

The first blow came from behind—a crushing impact to the back of her skull that sent her sprawling into the sand. She tried to get up, but another blow followed, then another. Something warm and wet was running down her face. Blood. So much blood.

Through the haze of pain, Lena saw that Roman was holding a hammer. He raised it again, and she managed to grab his wrist, the two of them wrestling for control of the weapon. But he was stronger, and when another blow connected with her head, her world tilted sideways.

Yet somehow, Lena found the strength to break away. She stumbled back toward where Beatriz lay bound in the sand. With shaking fingers, she managed to untie the ropes around her friend's ankles and wrists.

"Run!" Beatriz gasped. "Different directions!"

It was a desperate strategy, but it was all they had. If they split up, Roman could only chase one of them. Maybe one would escape. Maybe one could get help.

Beatriz disappeared into the scrubland while Lena ran across the open dunes. Behind them, they heard Roman roar in frustration. Then came a sound that chilled them both—the rumble of an engine starting up.

Roman had returned to his four-wheel drive vehicle.

———

Lena ran as hard as she could, but the sand made every step exhausting. Blood from her head wounds was getting in her eyes, making it hard to see. Behind her, she could hear the SUV's engine getting louder. She risked a glance back and saw the vehicle cresting a dune, Roman behind the wheel.

The first impact knocked her off her feet. The bull bar of the SUV slammed into her back, sending her tumbling across the sand. She tried to get up, but the vehicle was coming at her again. This time, she rolled to the side, barely avoiding the wheels.

Roman spun the SUV around for another pass. Lena knew she couldn't keep dodging forever. She was getting weaker, the blood loss making her dizzy. As the vehicle bore down on her again, she made a desperate decision.

Instead of trying to dodge, she ran toward the SUV.

At the last second, she jumped.

Her hands caught the bull bar, and momentum carried her up onto the hood. Roman slammed on the brakes, trying to throw her off, but Lena held on. She could see his face through the windshield, contorted with rage. He grabbed the hammer from the passenger seat and swung it at her through the open window.

Lena then pulled herself up onto the roof of the vehicle. Roman accelerated again, driving erratically through the dunes, trying to shake her off. She wrapped her fingers around the roof racks, holding on as the SUV bucked and lurched over the uneven terrain.

Then the engine died. The wheels spun uselessly in the soft sand. The vehicle was bogged.

Roman got out and stood beside the SUV, looking up at her. His demeanor had suddenly changed. The rage was gone, replaced by an eerie calm.

"Come down," he said. "I'm not going to hurt you."

"I can't trust you," Lena replied, her voice shaking. "You tried to kill me!"

Roman made a show of throwing the hammer away into the dunes, then the knife. "See? No weapons. Come down. You need medical attention."

Lena could feel herself getting weaker. The blood loss was severe. She could see the sun setting on the horizon, darkness approaching. If she stayed on the roof, she might pass out and fall. But if she came down…

Just then, she heard engines in the distance. Other vehicles.

Roman heard them too. He got back in the SUV and managed to get it moving again, driving slowly along the beach with Lena still on the roof. As they came around a bend, she saw them—three SUVs in the distance.

Roman stopped the vehicle.

Lena didn't hesitate. She slid off the roof and ran toward the other vehicles, leaving bloody footprints in the sand. Behind her, she heard Roman's engine start again, but she didn't look back.

———

The police arrived at Salt Creek two hours after Adam Stewart's emergency call. They found Roman Heinze sitting in his SUV among the dunes, the vehicle's interior and exterior covered in blood. He surrendered without resistance, but his eyes held no remorse.

Detective Sarah Chen from Major Crimes arrived the next morning to lead the investigation. What she found at the scene was deeply disturbing. The amount of blood in and on Roman's vehicle was extraordinary. Forensic analysts would later confirm the blood was Lena's, splattered across the roof, the hood, and inside the cabin. The DNA evidence was overwhelming.

When investigators executed a search warrant at Roman's home in the Adelaide suburb of Hackham, they discovered something even more disturbing. His computer contained hundreds of videos depicting violent rapes and sexual assaults. Browser histories showed an obsession with bondage and domination. This wasn't a spur-of-the-moment attack—this was a fantasy Roman had been nurturing for years.

As Detective Chen dug deeper into Roman's past, a pattern emerged. In 2014, he'd been convicted of indecently assaulting another female backpacker. He'd come up behind her in his home, placed his hand over her breast, and pushed her onto a bed. She'd fought him off and escaped, but Roman had received only a good behavior bond—with the specific condition that he not use electronic media to arrange meetings with people.

He'd violated that bond to contact Beatriz and Lena through Gumtree.

There were others, too. The investigation revealed that in the weeks leading up to the Salt Creek attack, Roman Heinze had contacted at least twelve other female backpackers through the website, offering them rides. They'd all declined or found other transportation. Lucky escapes, every one of them.

Then there was Sylvia Clarke, Roman's ex-girlfriend. When she saw news reports about the Salt Creek attack, she recognized his vehicle immediately. She'd been to Salt Creek with him before. She knew his patterns and had her own story to tell—one of violence and sexual assault that she'd reported to police, though Roman had never been convicted for it.

"If those fishermen hadn't been there," Sylvia told investigators, "he would have killed those girls. I know it."

Perhaps most chilling was a detail that emerged from locals at the Salt Creek roadhouse. Four years before the attack on Beatriz and Lena, witnesses remembered seeing Roman at the roadhouse with a young blonde woman who looked like a backpacker. Two days later, Roman left the area alone. The woman was never seen again.

Police launched a search of the dunes around Salt Creek, but the shifting sands revealed nothing. If there were other victims buried out there, the desert kept its secrets.

In the hospital, Beatriz and Lena were reunited. Both were traumatized, their bodies bearing the physical evidence of their ordeal. Lena had four deep lacerations on her scalp, one so severe that it exposed the skull bone beneath. The doctor told her that if the hammer blow had landed just a few centimeters to the side, it would have been fatal.

Beatriz's wrists and ankles showed deep ligature marks from the rope, and her face was swollen from Roman's punches. However, it was the psychological wounds that would take the longest to heal.

"You saved my life," Beatriz told Lena, gripping her hand.

"We saved each other," Lena replied.

As the investigation continued, more evidence piled up against Roman. The rope used to bind Beatriz still had his DNA on it. Forensic experts found Beatriz's saliva on her severed bikini, which Roman had used as a gag. His shirt was soaked with Lena's blood, front and back. Even a shovel among his camping equipment had Lena's blood on the handle—transferred there when Roman had tried to dig his vehicle out of the sand.

Detective Chen interviewed both women extensively. Their stories were consistent, their memories clear despite the trauma. They remembered details that would prove crucial—the sequence of events, the weapons used, Roman's words during the attack.

"He said he just wanted to try her," Lena recalled, the words still seeming impossible even as she spoke them.

The detective also interviewed the Mohammed family, the fishermen who'd rescued the women. Abdul-Karim described Beatriz's state when she'd run to their vehicle: "She looked like she had seen the devil himself."

His father, Ali, added another detail that would stick with investigators. When they'd first arrived at the scene to search for Lena, they'd noticed three men fishing nearby. The men could clearly hear the commotion—the screaming, the vehicle engines, and the chaos unfolding just beyond the dunes. Ali had shouted to them for help, gesturing frantically toward where the women were in danger. The men looked over but didn't move. They simply continued fishing. It later emerged that these three men were off-duty police officers. Their only contribution to the emergency, witnesses would report, was to drag some coolers across the beach entrance—possibly to block vehicle access—before returning to their fishing spots while two women fought for their lives nearby.

The trial began in March 2017 at the South Australian Supreme Court. Roman Heinze, now sixty-one years old, sat in the defendant's box looking small and pathetic—a far cry from the imposing figure who'd terrorized two women in the sand dunes.

Prosecutor Jim Pearce outlined the case in devastating detail. He walked the jury through the evidence—the DNA, the blood patterns, the weapons, and the rope. He showed them photographs of the crime scene, the abandoned campsite, and the blood-soaked vehicle.

But it was the testimony of Beatriz and Lena that truly conveyed the horror of what had happened at Salt Creek.

Beatriz took the stand first. Speaking through tears, she described the moment Roman's demeanor changed in the dunes, the terror of being bound and assaulted, the desperate struggle to survive.

"I felt like I was in a horror movie," she told the court. "I needed a strategy to get away."

The defense lawyer, Bill Boucaut, tried to undermine her credibility. He suggested she'd drunk too much wine, that perhaps she'd removed her bikini herself, that she'd fabricated the assault. Beatriz firmly rejected each suggestion, maintaining her account with unwavering consistency.

Lena testified the next day. She described waking to Beatriz's screams, confronting Roman, and the hammer blows that nearly killed her. She recounted the terrifying chase across the dunes, the desperate decision to jump onto the moving vehicle.

"He tried to kill me," she said simply. "Multiple times."

Boucaut attempted an even more absurd defense for Lena's injuries. Perhaps, he suggested, she'd climbed onto the vehicle's roof to look for her friend and had simply fallen off when the car had stopped suddenly. The jury members looked skeptical. The blood evidence alone made such a scenario impossible.

The defense's strategy seemed to be to cast doubt on the women's accounts, to suggest that things weren't as they seemed. Roman himself never testified. He sat silent throughout the trial, showing no emotion as his victims described their ordeal.

After twelve hours of deliberation, the jury returned their verdict: guilty on six charges, including indecent assault, aggravated kidnapping, and endangering life. They acquitted him on the charge of attempted murder, perhaps unable to prove beyond a reasonable doubt that he'd intended to kill rather than injure when he'd rammed Lena with his vehicle.

The sentencing hearing revealed more about Roman Heinze than the trial itself. Justice Trish Kelly had reviewed his history, his pattern of escalating violence, and his complete lack of remorse.

"Your conduct was utterly depraved," she told him. "You are not a civilized human being but an enraged and somewhat primitive man lacking any moral compass whatsoever."

She detailed how Roman's violence had been building for years. The 2014 assault, the obsession with violent pornography, and the systematic targeting of vulnerable young women through online platforms. Salt Creek was not an aberration—it was the culmination of a long descent into sadistic fantasy.

"If you had not been caught that day," Justice Kelly said, "your offending would have continued and quite probably escalated. You may well have killed someone."

She praised Beatriz and Lena for their courage and intelligence, noting that they had "outwitted and outsmarted" their attacker at every turn. She commended the Mohammed family and Adam Stewart for their heroic intervention. And, in a pointed aside that made headlines, she criticized the three off-duty police officers who'd been fishing nearby, noting that their only apparent contribution to the emergency was dragging coolers across the beach entrance before returning to their fishing while the attack continued.

Roman Heinze was sentenced to twenty-two years and four months in prison, with a non-parole period of seventeen years. Given his age, it was effectively a life sentence.

From his cell in Yatala Labour Prison, Roman has never accepted responsibility for his crimes. He continues to claim that Lena was never on the roof of his vehicle, despite photographic evidence, blood evidence, and multiple witness testimonies. He's filed appeal after appeal, all rejected. He even fought to prevent police from destroying his SUV, claiming he needed it preserved for future legal challenges.

His daughter, Kendehl, has spoken publicly about the impact of her father's crimes. She struggles to reconcile the father she thought she knew with the monster revealed at Salt Creek. From prison, Roman sends her threatening letters, demanding she "watch her back." Despite everything, she admits she still loves him, even as she fears what he might do if he's ever released.

For Beatriz and Lena, healing has been a long journey. Beatriz returned to Brazil but still struggles with darkness. She doesn't like to be outside after sunset. She feels paranoid when strangers walk behind her. A piece of her, she says, was stolen at Salt Creek.

Lena also returned home to Germany. She's found strength in survival, but the trauma remains. Both women credit each other with saving their lives that day in the dunes. Their bond, forged in unimaginable terror, remains strong.

Salt Creek itself has returned to its natural quiet. The wind still whispers through the coastal grass. The waves still crash against the pristine beach. However, for those who know what happened there in February 2016, it will never be just another beautiful stretch of Australian coastline.

It's a place where two young women faced a monster and survived through courage, intelligence, and sheer determination. Where ordinary fishermen became heroes. Where the veneer of safety was stripped away to reveal the predator lurking beneath.

Roman Heinze will be eligible for parole in 2033. He'll be seventy-seven years old. His victims, their families, and his own daughter all pray that day will never come. Because, as Justice Kelly noted in her sentencing remarks, Roman Heinze is a man without remorse, without rehabilitation, and without a moral compass.

He is, in the truest sense of the word, a monster.

CHAPTER 2
THE MIDDLETOWN NIGHTMARE

The winter darkness had already settled over Woodstock, Virginia, when the phone rang at the police station. It was after 10:00 p.m. on Sunday, January 22, 1995, and the caller's voice carried panic. A twelve-year-old girl had vanished from the Exxon station along Interstate 81. She'd gone to use the restroom and had never come back.

Woodstock police mobilized officers immediately. The temperature had plunged into the twenties, and every minute mattered. Search teams spread across the area surrounding the gas station, their flashlight beams cutting through the darkness. Dogs worked a mile radius, their handlers calling out the girl's name: Valerie Smelser.

The man who'd reported her missing, Norman Hoverter, told officers he'd been traveling with the girl's mother, Wanda Smelser, and her other children when Valerie had asked to use the bathroom. That was all. She just never came back out. Norman and Wanda joined the search briefly before telling officers they would drive around looking on their own. They loaded their two younger children into their car and disappeared into the night.

For two hours, search teams scoured ditches, checked dumpsters, and swept through nearby woods. The winter wind bit through their jackets as they called Valerie's name into the emptiness. No response came back.

———

Monday evening brought a different kind of cold to Clarke County, Virginia. A commuter driving along Route 50 near the Shenandoah River noticed something in a ravine off Route 638. He pulled over, walked closer through the winter debris, and then stumbled backward.

A child's nude body lay among the dead leaves and branches.

When Clarke County Sheriff's deputies arrived at the wooded ravine, the officers found themselves shaken. The child was severely emaciated, ribs protruding sharply through paper-thin skin, limbs like brittle sticks. One officer quietly told his partner the sight reminded him of documentary footage from World War II concentration camps.

By Tuesday morning, investigators had identified the body. This was Valerie Smelser, the girl reported missing from the Woodstock gas station—but she hadn't wandered off, and she hadn't been abducted by a stranger. The condition of her body told a different story entirely.

———

Virginia State Police Special Agent William Shevokas stood before the ramshackle frame house on Route 11 in Middletown, Frederick County, on Wednesday morning.

Paint peeled from the blue siding, and weeds choked the yard. This was the address Norman and Wanda had given to the police.

When Wanda answered his knock, Shevokas immediately noticed the other children. They huddled behind their mother, thin and dirty, their clothes stained and torn. Behind them, he could see into rooms piled with papers, rotting food, and debris stacked so high it nearly reached the ceiling. The smell hit him like a physical force: decay, mold, and something else. Something worse.

Norman sat silently in a corner of the cluttered living room while Shevokas asked about Valerie's disappearance. Their story matched what they'd told Woodstock police. The gas station. The bathroom. The vanishing. However, the fourteen-year-old girl behind Wanda was using a walker, and when Shevokas looked closer, he realized portions of her feet were missing. The seven-year-old boy also seemed unable to walk properly. When Norman stood to get something from another room, all three children flinched.

Shevokas requested permission to search the house. Wanda hesitated, glanced at Norman, and then nodded.

The investigator opened the basement door and immediately recoiled. The stench of human waste was overwhelming. His flashlight illuminated wooden steps caked with feces. As he descended into the darkness, each step revealed more horror. The dirt floor was covered in excrement and trash. He could see his breath in the freezing air. This basement had no heat, even in January.

Near the door, scratches covered the wood. Metal mounting points suggested some kind of restraint system had been attached there. In the corner sat a tin coffee can, its inside stained with old urine. Dark stains on the broken gypsum looked like dried blood.

This wasn't just a basement; it was a torture chamber.

———

On Thursday morning in the Frederick County Sheriff's Office interrogation room, Norman's story began to fall apart. Investigators pressed him about timeline inconsistencies. Why had they left the search scene so quickly? What about the condition of the house and the basement?

Norman's shoulders slumped. His voice dropped to barely a whisper.

"The statements made at the Woodstock gas station," he said, "were just a ruse."

The investigators leaned forward. Norman began to talk, but not to confess. According to him, he was just a bystander. Wanda made the rules. Wanda decided Valerie should live in the basement. He was too weak to stop her, too afraid to intervene.

But hours later, seven-year-old Benjamin told a different story. When Special Agent Shevokas asked him what life was like with Norman, the boy looked directly at him and spoke one word: "Hell."

Fourteen-year-old Brittany, despite her disability and trauma, found a way to communicate. Using a doll, she showed investigators how Norman kicked Valerie. How he punched her. How he tied her up. Her demonstrations were specific, detailed, and left no doubt about who had been the primary aggressor.

The evidence began to reveal what had happened on January 22, 1995.

That Sunday morning started like many others in the house on Route 11. Valerie had been in the basement for months by then, forced to use the tin can as a toilet, to sleep on the dirt floor amid her own waste. She weighed fifty-one pounds, about twenty pounds below normal for a twelve-year-old girl.

That morning, Valerie carried her waste can up from the basement. Her legs, weakened by starvation and cold, gave way. She tripped, and the can spilled across the kitchen floor.

Norman exploded. He grabbed Valerie and rubbed her face in the urine—and then the beating began. He slammed her head against the wall with such force that it punched through the drywall. He struck her head repeatedly with his fists. Finally, he kicked her down the basement stairs.

Norman found Wanda and bragged about how thoroughly he had beaten the child. However, Wanda didn't check on her daughter or call for help. She simply left Valerie lying in the freezing basement as the girl's brain swelled from the trauma.

By evening, Valerie was dead. Norman and Wanda wrapped up her emaciated body, drove to Clarke County, and dumped her in the ravine. Then they drove to Woodstock and made their false report, sending search teams looking in the wrong place for a girl who was already dead.

As investigators pieced together Valerie's story, the full horror emerged. For several months before her death, Valerie had been imprisoned in that basement. She was kept naked and chained to the door at night. She wasn't allowed to eat with the family or use the bathroom. Occasionally, someone would spray her with a hose in the backyard, which was the only form of bathing she received.

The autopsy revealed the extent of her suffering. Besides the fatal head trauma and hypothermia that killed her, Valerie showed evidence of long-term starvation, old fractures, and countless scars. The medical examiner also found evidence of sexual assault.

Brittany's missing feet told their own story. She had been forced to stand outside in freezing weather as punishment, resulting in frostbite so severe that amputation was necessary. Benjamin could barely walk from his own injuries. Four-year-old Nicholas, the youngest, had somehow survived with less physical damage, though the psychological scars ran deep.

The family had lived like this for years, moving constantly to avoid detection. Wanda had relocated her children through more than half a dozen jurisdictions across Virginia and West Virginia over five years. Each time social services received a complaint, the family would vanish. Valerie's father, Loyd Sr., had tried repeatedly to report suspected abuse, as had her uncle, Lee.

The complaints never resulted in action. The family would simply disappear.

Wanda had claimed religious exemption from public schooling, keeping the children invisible to teachers who might have noticed the abuse. She had requested a homeschooling application but never submitted it. There were no doctors' visits, no checkups. No one at all could see what was happening behind the closed doors of the house on Route 11.

On January 26, 1995, Norman Hoverter and Wanda Smelser were charged with first-degree murder. The surviving children were placed in protective custody. For the first time in years, Brittany, Benjamin, and Nicholas were safe.

As the legal proceedings began, both defendants tried to blame the other. Norman's attorney painted him as a weak man dominated by Wanda. Norman claimed he was too afraid of her to intervene, too in love to leave—but the evidence told a different story. The children's testimony, the physical evidence, and the pattern of abuse all pointed to Norman as the primary aggressor.

Wanda's defense took the opposite approach. Her attorney argued she was a battered woman, dominated by an abusive and sadistic man. A psychological evaluation labeled Norman an "egocentric psychopath." According to this narrative, Wanda had been paralyzed by fear, unable to protect her daughter.

The legal proceedings moved swiftly by judicial standards. In July 1995, Norman entered an Alford plea to first-degree murder and abduction. This meant he maintained his innocence while acknowledging the prosecution had enough evidence to convict him. He tried to withdraw the plea weeks later, claiming he'd been tricked, but the judge found no evidence of deception.

On August 31, 1995, Norman stood for sentencing. Commonwealth's Attorney Lawrence Ambrogi didn't hold back: "If there ever was a case that deserved the maximum penalty, this is the case." He called the treatment of Valerie "sadistic, savage, and inhumane."

Norman wept as he addressed the court, still refusing to accept responsibility. Through his tears, he continued to blame Wanda, insisting that if given another chance, he would have taken things more into his own hands. His statement suggested Wanda had been in control, a claim that contradicted all the evidence presented.

Judge James L. Berry was unmoved by Norman's tears or his attempts to shift blame. He handed down the maximum sentence: life in prison for first-degree murder, plus a concurrent ten-year suspended sentence for abduction. Under Virginia law at the time, Norman would be eligible for geriatric parole after serving ten years, when he turned sixty. Given the heinous nature of his crimes, early release seemed unlikely; the fifty-year-old would almost certainly die behind bars.

Wanda's case resolved differently. In August 1996, on the morning her trial was to begin, she pleaded no contest to reduced charges of second-degree murder and abduction. The plea deal had been crafted for a specific reason: to spare Brittany from testifying against her mother. The traumatized, disabled fifteen-year-old simply could not endure that ordeal.

At her sentencing in October 1996, Wanda sobbed as she spoke: "I realize now I should have done more to stop Norman. At the time, I couldn't think straight."

The judge sentenced her to twelve years in prison. Some felt it was too lenient for a mother who had allowed her child to be tortured and killed. Others saw a broken woman paying for her weakness and failure.

The Valerie Smelser case exposed critical failures in Virginia's child protection system. The religious exemption loophole, the lack of coordination between counties, and the absence of mandatory health checks for homeschooled children had all contributed to Valerie's invisibility and death.

Some reforms followed. Virginia tightened regulations and improved inter-agency communication, but advocates argued the changes weren't enough. Too many children could still disappear from view, hidden behind religious exemptions and frequent moves.

The surviving Smelser children began long roads to recovery with relatives. The house on Route 11 stood empty for months before new tenants moved in, unaware or unconcerned about its history. The gas station in Woodstock continued serving travelers, most never knowing it had been the starting point of an elaborate lie.

For those who worked the case, Valerie's story became a permanent weight. Special Agent Shevokas called the basement scene the worst thing he'd encountered in his career, and the Commonwealth's Attorney Ambrogi kept Valerie's photograph in his office as a reminder.

In November 1996, the Virginia Court of Appeals upheld Norman's conviction and life sentence. He would die in prison. Wanda would serve her twelve years and return to a world where she would forever be known as the mother who let her daughter die.

Valerie Smelser was twelve years old when she died. She spent her final months chained in a basement, starved, beaten, and forced to live in her own waste. She needed teachers to notice her absence, doctors to see her injuries, and social workers to pursue her case across county lines. Most of all, she needed a mother who would protect her.

Instead, she got Norman's fists and Wanda's indifference. She got a system that let her disappear and a community that didn't know she existed until she was gone.

CHAPTER 3
THE BODY IN THE GARDEN

Michelle James stood on her patio in the Welsh village of Beddau, scissors in hand, staring at the bulky package wrapped in gray plastic. It was November 24, 2015, a cold morning that carried the promise of winter. Her friend Rhian stood beside her, both women preparing for what they thought would be a harmless prank.

The package had belonged to their recently deceased neighbor, Leigh Ann Sabine, who everyone called Lee. The eccentric seventy-four-year-old had died from brain cancer nearly a month earlier, leaving behind this mysterious bundle she'd always claimed was a medical skeleton from her nursing days. Lee had even asked Michelle to use it to scare the next tenants—one final joke from beyond the grave.

Michelle cut through the first layer of plastic. Then another. And another. The wrapping seemed endless, layer upon layer of shopping bags, bin liners, and roofing felt. She and Rhian exchanged glances, their amusement turning to puzzlement. Why would anyone wrap a teaching skeleton this thoroughly?

They'd counted forty-one layers when Michelle's scissors finally broke through to something different. A foul stench erupted from the opening, overwhelming and unmistakable—the smell of death. Through the tear in the plastic, she glimpsed not the white of medical bones but something brown and preserved, wrapped in blue-striped pajamas.

Michelle dropped the scissors and stumbled backward.

"It's a dead body!" she screamed. "It's a dead body!"

Rhian fumbled for her phone while Michelle ran inside, her hands shaking. The prank had become a nightmare. What they'd discovered on that ordinary Tuesday morning would unravel one of Britain's most extraordinary murder cases—a crime that had remained hidden for eighteen years, concealed by a woman who'd lived among them, hosted their barbecues, read their tarot cards, and kept her terrible secret wrapped in plastic just meters from where children played.

———

Three months before the discovery, Leigh Ann Sabine had been the life of Trem-y-Cwm, the small complex of council flats where she'd lived since 1997. At seventy-four, she still wore fishnet stockings and bright lipstick; her hair bleached blond or dyed an impossible shade of red. Neighbors would see her in the communal garden she'd transformed into what she called her "little piece of paradise," cigarette in one hand, gin and tonic in the other, holding court with her stories.

Leigh Ann Sabine

She had so many stories. Lee claimed she'd been a cabaret singer in Australia, a model in her youth, a millionaire's ex-wife. Her accent was theatrical, cultivated—definitely not Welsh, though she'd grown up in the nearby village of Gelli, something she rarely mentioned. She preferred to tell people she was from New Zealand or Australia, exotic places that matched her carefully constructed persona.

Mary Gardner, who lived in the same complex, found Lee fascinating and frustrating in equal measure. The two women would sit in the garden for hours, Lee spinning tales while Mary listened with a mixture of entertainment and skepticism. There was something about Lee that didn't quite add up. Her flat contained no family photos, no mementos of the rich life she claimed to have lived. Just one black-and-white glamour shot from her younger days, when she'd supposedly performed under the name Lee Martin.

"Watch out, or I'll frog you," Lee would joke when someone annoyed her, a strange phrase that made the neighbors laugh. She had peculiar expressions like that, remnants of a life lived elsewhere, or perhaps nowhere at all.

The summer of 2015 brought changes. Lee suffered a fall that led to a hospital visit, where doctors delivered devastating news: brain cancer, advanced and inoperable. Lynne Williams, a fifty-four-year-old cleaning business owner, met Lee at the Royal Glamorgan Hospital and took pity on the dying woman who seemed to have no visitors. Lynne began visiting daily, bringing cigarettes and home-cooked meals, listening to Lee's increasingly fragmented stories.

"I've got a secret," Lee told Lynne one day, her eyes glittering with what might have been mischief or malice. However, when Lynne pressed for details, Lee changed the subject, as she always did when conversation veered too close to something real.

In her final weeks, Lee made an unusual request. She gathered Lynne and Michelle in her flat, her voice weak but insistent. "There's a skeleton in the shed," she said. "After I'm gone, move it to the attic. Scare the next tenants." She grinned, showing teeth stained by decades of cigarettes.

"I hope it's not a bloody real one," Lynne had joked.

Lee had pointed a finger tipped with bright orange nail polish and said, "You never know."

They'd laughed it off. Everything with Lee was performance and drama, stories that might or might not be true. Even dying, she couldn't resist one last theatrical gesture.

Leigh Ann Sabine died on October 30, 2015. Her funeral at Glyntaff Crematorium was small but warm, attended by the neighbors who'd become her only family. Mary West, a street pastor who'd tried to bring Lee comfort in her final months, delivered the eulogy. She spoke of a complicated woman who loved Radio 4, argued about everything, and never quite told the truth about anything.

None of them knew they'd just cremated a murderer.

―――

Police Community Support Officer Gareth Bishop arrived at Trem-y-Cwm within minutes of the emergency call. The smell hit him before he even reached the patio—rotting waste, like a compost bin left too long in summer heat. Michelle James stood in her doorway, visibly shaking, while Rhian waited by the package they'd abandoned on the concrete.

PC Joy Nicholls arrived shortly after. She'd known Lee over the years, had dealt with the occasional complaint about noise from her barbecues. Lee had been likeable but untrustworthy, the kind of person who told different stories to different people. Now Nicholls stared at what Lee had left behind: a body wrapped so thoroughly it had taken two women with garden shears and kitchen knives to breach its plastic cocoon.

The scene was immediately sealed. Forensics teams descended on the quiet cul-de-sac, their white suits stark against the Welsh gray. Neighbors gathered at the police tape, whispering. Beddau hadn't seen a murder in twenty years.

Within hours, South Wales Police had a suspect in custody: Michelle James herself. She'd been found with the body, and she had admitted to cutting it open. The initial hypothesis seemed straightforward—a falling out between neighbors, perhaps over Lee's estate. Michelle was taken to the station in handcuffs, her protests of innocence falling on professionally skeptical ears.

Detective Chief Inspector Gareth Morgan took charge of the investigation. The first priority was identifying the body. The remains were remarkably preserved, mummified by the layers of plastic that had created an airless tomb. The corpse still wore blue-striped pajamas with a Marks & Spencer label that read "St. Michael"—a brand name the store had discontinued in 2000.

While Michelle sat in a cell, convinced she was about to be charged with a murder she hadn't committed, Morgan's team began unraveling the truth. They started with Leigh Ann Sabine herself. Who was this woman who'd died claiming to own a medical skeleton?

———

The tenancy records for the flat revealed something interesting. In February 1997, the lease had been signed by two people: Leigh Ann Sabine and John Henry Sabine. A year later, John's name had been removed. Where was John Sabine?

A search of death records turned up nothing. No death certificate, no cremation record, no burial. According to official documents, John Sabine should have been 85 years old, but no one in Beddau had ever seen him. Mary Gardner had lived in the complex for over a decade and had never known

Lee had a husband. Michelle James, who'd been Lee's neighbor and informal carer, had always assumed she was widowed or divorced.

The investigators dug deeper. John Sabine had registered with a local general practitioner in 1997, shortly after moving to Beddau. In April of that year, he'd requested a prescription refill. The prescription was never collected. After that, John Sabine had simply vanished from all records except one—he'd continued to appear on the electoral register, and his pension had continued to be paid into a joint account that Leigh Ann accessed.

The body in the plastic began to tell its own story. Dr. Richard Jones, the forensic pathologist, found evidence of severe trauma to the skull. Multiple fractures radiated from the base of the cranium, consistent with blunt force trauma. This was no natural death. John Sabine—if this was John Sabine—had been murdered.

DNA would confirm the identification, but the police needed a comparison sample. The search for John Sabine's relatives began, complicated by the decades that had passed and the false trails Leigh Ann had laid. She'd told neighbors various stories about her husband—that he'd abandoned her for another woman, that he'd been abusive, that he'd returned to New Zealand. All lies, the investigators were beginning to realize, designed to explain an absence that had lasted eighteen years.

While forensics teams processed the scene in Beddau, Detective Chief Inspector Morgan's investigation expanded beyond Wales. The tenancy records showed that John and

Leigh Ann had moved to Beddau from somewhere else. But where? And, more importantly, who were these people?

The breakthrough came from an unexpected source. Following media appeals for information about John Sabine, Christopher, a farmer from Northamptonshire, contacted the police. He was John Sabine's son from a first marriage—a relationship that had ended when John had left his first wife for a young nurse named Leigh Ann in the late 1950s. Christopher hadn't seen his father in 27 years but agreed to provide a DNA sample.

The match was conclusive. The body wrapped in plastic was John Henry Sabine, born around 1930, a Korean War veteran who'd worked as an accountant before his disappearance. Christopher's statement to police painted a picture of a man he barely knew, a father who'd abandoned his first family for a woman Christopher called "evil."

However, the Sabine story went deeper than a simple affair and remarriage. As investigators traced the couple's history, they uncovered something that stunned detectives: John and Leigh Ann Sabine had abandoned five children in New Zealand in 1969.

The discovery came through international police cooperation. New Zealand authorities had records of a notorious case from 1969 when five children—Susan, Steven, Martin, Jane, and Lee-Ann Sabine, aged between two and eleven—had been left at an Auckland nursery. Their parents had told staff they were going shopping, but they never returned.

The abandonment had been national news in New Zealand. The children had spent the next decade in foster care, some experiencing abuse that would scar them for life. The parents, meanwhile, had fled to Australia, where Leigh Ann pursued dreams of cabaret stardom under the stage name Lee Martin.

The investigators tracked down the abandoned children, now adults in their fifties and sixties, scattered across New Zealand and beyond. Their statements revealed a pattern of cruelty that contextualized the murder. Jane Sabine, the second youngest, was blunt: "My mother was a nasty, horrible, heartless bitch." Her brother, Steve, was more analytical but no less damning: "If anyone was going to do it, she was going to do it. My father was actually a good man, a softhearted man. But she was a conniving bitch."

In 1984, the parents had attempted a reunion with their children, returning to New Zealand after fifteen years. The reunion had lasted mere months. When Jane confronted her mother about the abandonment, Leigh Ann had flown into what Jane described as an "incandescent" rage.

"I don't feel we owe you an explanation," she'd told her daughter.

Shortly after, when Jane and Lee-Ann brought a television reporter to the house to expose their parents' return, John and Leigh Ann vanished again, this time returning to Britain.

Steve Sabine remembered watching his mother's rage during that confrontation. "I looked at her, and I thought, 'My God, she could kill someone.'" His words, spoken to investigators in 2015, carried the weight of tragic prophecy.

Back in Wales, the investigation was uncovering evidence that Leigh Ann Sabine had been confessing to murder for years—she just hadn't been believed.

Valerie Chalkley came forward with a story that made investigators' blood run cold. In 1997, shortly after John's disappearance, Leigh Ann had called her out of the blue. "I've killed him," she'd announced. "I've battered him with a stone frog, which was at the side of the bed. He was just driving me mad. Every night, he would get into bed crying and weeping, saying, 'You don't fancy me.'"

Valerie had thought it was another of Lee's dramatic stories. Lee was always saying outrageous things, making up tales for attention. Valerie had laughed it off, though something had made her call back later to check. Lee had been dismissive, changing the subject. Valerie had let it go. Now, eighteen years later, she sat in a police interview room, realizing she'd heard a genuine confession to murder and done nothing.

She wasn't the only one. Bernadette Adamiec, a Beddau hairdresser, recalled an incident from early 2000. She'd been giving Lee a tarot reading—Lee loved anything mystical and theatrical—when her client had suddenly blurted out that she was going to be "famous...because of the body in the bag." Bernadette had laughed. Everyone laughed at Lee's stories.

The pattern became clear. Leigh Ann Sabine had been playing a psychological game for almost two decades, telling the truth in a way that sounded like lies. She'd hidden her crime in plain sight, wrapped in layers of eccentricity and performance, just as she'd wrapped John's body in layers of plastic.

The murder weapon surfaced through another of Lee's "jokes." Multiple neighbors remembered her strange phrase: "Watch out, or I'll frog you." It had seemed like nonsense, another of Mad Lee's peculiarities…but when investigators searched for the stone frog Valerie Chalkley had described, they found it. A neighbor had been given the ornament by

Lee before her death—a 2.5-pound ceramic frog, 14 centimeters long, with a protruding eye and hind leg.

Dr. Richard Jones examined the frog alongside photographs of John Sabine's skull fractures. The match was precise. The protruding features of the ornament aligned perfectly with the trauma patterns. This kitschy garden decoration, the kind found in countless British gardens, had been used to beat a man to death.

The investigation revealed more about that night in 1997. John had been drinking but was below the legal limit for driving—he hadn't been incapacitated. He'd been wearing pajamas, suggesting he'd been in bed or preparing for bed. Finally, the fractures indicated multiple blows to the back of the head. John Sabine likely hadn't seen his death coming.

The forensic analysis of John's body revealed something extraordinary about his preservation. The combination of materials Leigh Ann had used—plastic bags, roofing felt, cardboard, tin foil—had created conditions that prevented normal decomposition. The body had undergone what Dr. Jones termed "chemical mummification."

The wrapping had been methodical and obsessive. Investigators counted layer after layer, some dating from the late 1990s based on the shopping bags used, others clearly added later. The body had been moved multiple times. Initially, evidence suggested it had been stored in the flat itself, possibly in a platform bed in the spare room. At some point, before Leigh Ann's death, it had been relocated to the garden shed and placed beneath a potting table, which was where Michelle would go on to discover it.

The physical effort involved was considerable. John Sabine had been a full-grown man. Leigh Ann, even in 1997, had been in her mid-fifties. How had she managed not just to kill him but to wrap the body so thoroughly and move it repeatedly over eighteen years?

The answer seemed to lie in Leigh Ann's nursing background. She understood bodies, decomposition, and preservation. The wrapping technique—particularly the use of roofing felt to absorb moisture while plastic prevented air circulation—suggested knowledge of how to prevent the telltale signs of death from escaping. No neighbors had ever complained of smells. No one had noticed anything amiss during the various moves between tenancies and flat inspections.

The financial motive became clearer as investigators examined bank records. For eighteen years, Leigh Ann had collected John's army pension and state benefits, money paid into their joint account that she accessed freely. She'd removed his name from the tenancy in 1998 to qualify for single-occupancy benefits while maintaining his presence on the electoral register to avoid triggering an investigation into his whereabouts.

The investigators uncovered a letter Leigh Ann had written to her daughter, Jane, a year before her death. The language was bizarre, threatening: "Like the phoenix, I will arise from the ashes and sleep will obey me and visit thee never. For my eyes are upon thee, forever and ever. I have served my life sentence of shame and blame. Now it is your turn to do the same." She'd signed it: "Your nemesis, Ann Lee Sabine."

Even facing death from cancer, Leigh Ann had remained vindictive toward the children who'd exposed her in 1984, the ones who'd dared to challenge her carefully constructed lies.

———

As the investigation progressed, a psychological profile of Leigh Ann Sabine emerged that was as fascinating as it was disturbing. Everyone who'd known her had a different version of Lee. To some, she was a harmless eccentric, the kind of colorful character who enlivened a quiet Welsh village. To others, she was a compulsive liar whose stories grew more elaborate with each telling. To her children, she was a monster who'd abandoned them twice and never shown a moment of remorse.

Mary West, the street pastor who'd tried to comfort Lee in her final months, struggled to reconcile the woman she'd known with the murderer being revealed. Lee had been intelligent and well-read, an avid Radio 4 listener who loved to debate. She'd also been utterly without genuine emotional connections.

The investigation revealed that even Lee's basic identity was partly fabricated. She'd claimed to be from New Zealand or Australia, but records showed she'd been born in Gelli, Wales, as the daughter of a miner. Her exotic accent, her stories of international adventure—all carefully constructed lies designed to distance herself from her ordinary origins.

Detective Chief Inspector Morgan characterized her as "an absolute storyteller" whose "stories of her life were totally mythical." But the lies went deeper than mere self-aggrandizement; they were a means of control, a way to manipulate reality to suit her needs. When John became inconvenient—his crying, his regrets about the abandoned children, his very existence—she'd eliminated him and created a new story to explain his absence.

The fact that she'd lived with his body for eighteen years suggested something beyond mere criminality. Most killers who conceal bodies do so out of necessity, disposing of them when possible. Leigh Ann had kept John close, moving him from room to room, maintaining him like a macabre possession. Some investigators wondered if she'd enjoyed the secret, the power of knowing something no one else did.

Her final actions suggested she'd wanted the truth to emerge after her death. Why else tell Michelle about the "skeleton"? Why make such a point of ensuring someone would find it? Perhaps she'd wanted the fame she'd always craved—or perhaps it was one final act of cruelty, ensuring that Michelle, who'd cared for her in her final months, would be traumatized by the discovery.

———

After forty-eight hours in custody, Michelle James was released without charge. The DNA results had confirmed the body was John Sabine, who'd died around 1997, when Michelle hadn't even lived in Beddau. The physical evidence —Leigh Ann's hair found in the wrapping, her fingerprints on the materials—all pointed to the dead woman as the sole perpetrator.

However, freedom didn't end Michelle's ordeal. She returned to Trem-y-Cwm to find her life transformed. Some neighbors supported her, understanding she'd been another of Lee's victims. Others whispered, wondered, and questioned how she couldn't have known. The image of the body, the smell, the feeling of fluid on her hands as she'd cut through the plastic—these haunted her. She developed PTSD, requiring therapy to process the trauma.

"Why didn't she confess?" Michelle asked investigators, journalists, and anyone who would listen. "She knew she was dying. She knew what she was doing to me. She is still doing it to me. Why?"

There was no answer. Leigh Ann Sabine had taken her motivations to her grave, leaving behind only questions and trauma.

With the perpetrator dead, there could be no criminal trial. Instead, the case proceeded to a coroner's inquest to formally determine the cause of John Sabine's death. In May 2016, Senior Coroner Andrew Barkley presided over the hearing at Aberdare Coroner's Court.

The evidence was overwhelming. Dr. Richard Jones testified about the skull fractures and their match to the stone frog. Valerie Chalkley recounted the confession she'd dismissed as fantasy. Detective Chief Inspector Morgan presented the financial evidence, the pattern of deception, the eighteen years of lies.

Christopher Sabine, John's son from his first marriage, provided a victim impact statement. He called Leigh Ann "an evil woman" who had "told a pack of lies all her life." He'd spent twenty-seven years wondering if his father was alive or dead. Now he knew.

The abandoned children from New Zealand weren't present, but their statements were read. They painted a picture of a woman without conscience, capable of abandoning her own children without remorse and then murdering the husband who'd shown regret for that abandonment.

Coroner Barkley's verdict was unequivocal: unlawful killing. John Sabine had been murdered, and while the court couldn't prosecute a dead woman, the record would show that Leigh Ann Sabine was responsible for his death.

"Precisely what happened and the circumstances will sadly never totally be known," Barkley said. "But it is without doubt that foul play was the cause of death."

―――――

It was almost the perfect murder. The clues had been there all along—the confessions dismissed as jokes, the absent husband no one questioned, the mysterious package she talked about too often. Leigh Ann had hidden in plain sight, protected by her eccentricity and the human tendency to dismiss the outrageous as impossible.

She'd wanted to be famous after death, she'd told her hairdresser. In that, at least, Leigh Ann Sabine had told the truth.

CHAPTER 4
THE DEATH DEAL

The black Dodge station wagon had been sitting there for hours, engine cold, windows fogged with condensation in the humid July darkness. Anyone passing by on East 120th Street might have assumed someone was sleeping it off, maybe pulled over after a long night. As dawn broke over the Wagner Houses on July 16, 2009, the truth that emerged was far more disturbing.

Inside the vehicle, a man sat rigid behind the steering wheel, held upright by a telephone wire wrapped around both his neck and the headrest. His white dress shirt, once crisp and professional, was now a canvas of dark red, soaked through with blood that had pooled in his lap and spilled onto the gray interior. More wire bound his wrists behind his back. Seven stab wounds clustered in a six-inch area of his chest, each one precise, each one fatal. They had punctured his heart, lungs, liver, and aorta.

At 6:15 a.m., a resident of the Wagner Houses called 911 about the suspicious vehicle parked on Paladino Avenue, between First and Second Avenues. This wasn't the kind of neighborhood where nice cars sat unattended overnight—not without consequences.

The first patrol officers arrived within minutes, their flashlights cutting through the morning gloom as they approached the Dodge. One look through the driver's side window, and they knew this was no drunk sleeping it off. The crime scene tape went up fast, yellow barriers against the curious morning crowd already gathering on the sidewalk.

The victim's driver's license, found in the glove compartment among scattered business cards, identified him as Jeffrey Locker, fifty-two years old, from North Woodmere on Long Island. The business cards read "Jeffrey Locker - Motivational Speaker - Bringing Spirituality into the Business World." North Woodmere was thirty miles away, a world apart from this corner of East Harlem. What had brought this suburban businessman to these streets in the dead of night?

The scene told a confusing story. This looked like a carjacking, maybe a robbery gone wrong. The victim's wallet was missing—but then why was the car still here? Why hadn't they taken the vehicle? And there was something else that didn't fit: Despite the massive trauma and the blood-soaked clothing, the steering wheel and dashboard remained remarkably clean. It was as if Jeffrey had been positioned after the wounds were inflicted, not during a struggle.

―――――

Two detectives made the drive out to Long Island that morning, watching the city transform into suburbs through their windshield. They found the Locker home on a tree-lined street in North Woodmere, the kind of place where lawn services arrived on schedule and every driveway held at least two cars.

Lois Locker answered the door in her robe, her teenage children gathered behind her in the hallway. The detectives delivered the news with practiced gentleness, explaining that Jeffrey had been found deceased in East Harlem, and they were investigating the circumstances.

What happened next would stick with both detectives for years.

The widow and her children received the news without gasps, tears, or any collapse of grief. Lois simply nodded, as if confirming something she already knew. Their daughter announced she was going back to bed. The family stood there in their doorway, composed and calm, receiving news of a violent death like they were being told about a delayed flight.

When detectives asked about their last contact with Jeffrey, Lois mentioned he had called the previous night, claiming to have a flat tire.

The entire interaction lasted less than fifteen minutes. As the detectives walked back to their car, both noted how unusual the family's composure seemed, later describing to colleagues their feeling that the family had somehow been expecting this news.

Back in Manhattan, the investigation was moving fast. Within hours of finding Jeffrey's body, detectives discovered his ATM card had been used multiple times. The first withdrawal had happened at 6:45 a.m., just thirty minutes after the body was discovered. Security footage from a corner store ATM showed a tall Black man in a white t-shirt punching in the PIN without hesitation.

This wasn't the behavior of a typical thief with a stolen card. No looking around nervously. No attempt to hide his face. The man entered the code casually, collected his cash, and walked out like he was running a routine errand. Over the next several hours, he appeared at five different ATMs throughout East Harlem. Three hundred dollars here, two hundred there, staying below transaction limits while accumulating $1,100 total.

The quality of the footage was better than usual. One corner store had recently upgraded its security system after a string of robberies, and the man's face was clearly visible. At one location, he even stopped to buy a soda after making his withdrawal.

Then things got strange. Crime scene technicians processing Jeffrey's car found nearly $7,000 in cash stuffed into various pockets and compartments throughout the vehicle. Different denominations, some bills crisp and new, others worn and wrinkled. Some were visible in the cup holder, others protruding from the center console.

If this were a robbery, why take an ATM card worth maybe a thousand dollars but leave seven thousand in cash?

———

Five days of old-fashioned police work paid off. Detectives canvassed East Harlem with printouts from the ATM footage. A home health aide recognized the man immediately. "That's Kenny Minor," she said. "He's been around here forever."

Kenneth Minor was thirty-eight years old, once a promising computer technician who'd spiraled into addiction after losing his job. His record showed arrests for drugs, petty theft, and robbery. The resume of someone whose life had taken too many wrong turns.

On July 21, police officers found Kenneth at an apartment building six blocks from where Jeffrey's body was discovered. He was staying with a cousin, sleeping on the couch. When the police knocked at 6:00 a.m., Kenneth was already awake. He neither ran nor resisted, and as they cuffed him, one officer noted that he seemed almost relieved.

At the precinct, Kenneth sat silent for hours while detectives laid out their case. They had him on video using the dead man's ATM card at five locations, and they had witnesses who could identify him. This was murder during a robbery, they said. That meant life in prison. Maybe they could work something out if he cooperated.

For ten hours, Kenneth said nothing beyond asking for water and bathroom breaks. Then, as hour eleven began, he looked up and spoke four words that changed everything:

"This was a Kevorkian."

The detective conducting the interrogation paused. "Kevorkian? Like Doctor Jack Kevorkian?"

Kenneth nodded. "The suicide doctor. That's what this was. The man wanted to die."

What followed was one of the most extraordinary confessions in NYPD history.

According to Kenneth, the truth was more disturbing than any robbery gone wrong. Around 3:00 a.m. on July 16, Jeffrey Locker had been cruising East Harlem in his Dodge station wagon, but he wasn't lost. He was shopping—shopping for someone desperate enough to kill him.

Kenneth had been standing outside a 24-hour deli, coming down from a cocaine high, when the Dodge had pulled up to the curb. The driver had rolled down his window. A middle-aged white man in business clothes, completely out of place.

"I thought he was a cop," Kenneth explained to detectives. "White guy asking about guns at three in the morning? I told him to get lost."

But Jeffrey had kept circling the block. Three times he came back. On the third approach, he was direct: "I want you to shoot me."

Kenneth described Jeffrey's desperation, the words tumbling out in a rush. Jeffrey was drowning in debt from a Ponzi scheme while his business had collapsed, leaving his credit cards maxed out and bankruptcy looming on the horizon. But he had life insurance worth millions that would save his family. The policies wouldn't pay for suicide, especially the new ones he'd just bought. It had to look like a murder. Like a robbery.

"He had it all figured out," Kenneth told the detectives. Jeffrey gave him the ATM card and told him the PIN: 1322. Jeffrey instructed him to use the card afterward to establish a robbery motive. However, Jeffrey warned him not to take the large amount of cash in the car—taking thousands in cash plus the ATM card would trigger a more intensive murder investigation. It needed to look like a quick street robbery where the attacker grabbed only what was easiest.

The killing method evolved through negotiation. Jeffrey wanted to be shot, but Kenneth didn't have a gun. Finally, Jeffrey remembered a knife in his glove compartment. He instructed Kenneth to tear the phone wire from an apartment building vestibule to tie him up. Make it look authentic.

"Then came the worst part," Kenneth said, his voice dropping.

Kenneth explained that he'd held the knife blade against the steering wheel while Jeffrey threw himself forward onto it. Four times. Then Jeffrey told him to move the knife to the right, toward his heart. Two more times, maybe three.

"When I left, he was still breathing," Kenneth said. "He made these gurgling sounds. But he looked at me. Not scared. It was almost like he had a smirk on his face."

Kenneth's bizarre story might have been dismissed as the desperate fantasy of a caught killer, except for what happened next. As news of the arrest spread through East Harlem, a fifty-five-year-old con man named Melvin Fleming contacted his lawyer. Fleming had information that would prove Kenneth was telling the truth.

About a week before his death, Jeffrey had found Fleming and made the same proposition. "Make me dead," Jeffrey had said. Those exact words. It had to look like a robbery. The body had to be found.

Fleming, sensing opportunity, had played along. Over two nights, he'd driven around Harlem with Jeffrey, scouting locations. The bus terminal. A parking garage. Finally, the area around the Wagner Houses. Jeffrey was methodical, thinking through every detail. Time of night. Witnesses. How long before the body would be discovered.

Jeffrey had paid Fleming about $2,000 in cash upfront, plus jewelry to pawn. He'd even provided two switchblade knives. "If you don't want to shoot me," Jeffrey had said, "you can use these."

On their second meeting, Fleming told Jeffrey to wait in his car at the Wagner Houses while he went to get a gun. Instead, Fleming walked away with the money. He'd taken nearly $7,000 total from Jeffrey, leaving him desperate and broke, still searching for someone to help him die.

"I figured he'd give up," Fleming said. "Go home. Get help. I didn't think he'd find someone else."

As detectives dug into Jeffrey's life, they uncovered a man in financial freefall. The successful motivational speaker who taught corporations about handling stress was drowning in his own.

In January 2009, Jeffrey's bank account held $87,000. By July, just $5,800 remained. The recession had destroyed his speaking business when corporations had slashed training budgets. However, the real catastrophe had come in April, when a federal bankruptcy trustee had sued him for $1,210,200 in "bogus profits" from Lou Pearlman's $300 million Ponzi scheme. Pearlman, who'd created the

Backstreet Boys and NSYNC, had built a massive fraud empire that collapsed in 2007.

Jeffrey had claimed innocence, said he was just another duped investor, but the trustee had wanted the money back regardless. In a desperate letter to the bankruptcy court, Jeffrey wrote: "I am severely in credit card debt and my business is just paying my family's bills." Bankruptcy would destroy his career. Who would hire a bankrupt motivational speaker?

Digital forensics revealed Jeffrey's final desperate gambit. In his last months, he'd purchased approximately $14 million in new life insurance policies, adding to $4 million in existing coverage. On one application, he'd claimed an annual income of $800,000. His real income was less than $225,000.

He'd researched funeral arrangements online and sent his wife detailed emails about protecting assets from creditors, repeatedly using the phrase "when I am gone." His computer history showed visits to life insurance websites, specifically checking suicide exclusion clauses and contestability periods.

The plan was elaborate, calculated, and desperate. It had only required one final element: someone like Kenneth Minor.

———

The case that went to trial in February 2011 was unlike anything Manhattan's courts had seen. During jury selection, potential jurors kept admitting they couldn't convict someone for helping another person die. It took three days to find twelve people willing to follow the law regardless of personal feelings.

Prosecutor Peter Casolaro acknowledged the strangeness while insisting the law was clear: "Jeffrey Locker was a foolish, dishonest, pathetic man. But Kenneth Minor is a vicious and callous one. Being paid to kill another person, even if that person is the one paying you, makes you nothing more than a contract killer and a murderer."

Defense attorney Daniel Gotlin painted a different picture: "He didn't go to Park Avenue. He didn't go to Sutton Place. He went to the ghetto. And he did it more than once until he could find the right sucker to help him end his life."

When Melvin Fleming took the stand, his testimony devastated the prosecution's murder theory while somehow making Kenneth look worse. Asked why he didn't kill Jeffrey despite taking his money, Fleming's answer was brutal in its simplicity: "I'm a con man, not a killer. There's a difference."

The defense brought in Dr. Cyril Wecht, the forensic pathologist who'd worked on everything from JFK to JonBenet Ramsey. Using a mannequin, Wecht demonstrated how someone could impale themselves on a held knife with enough force to create Jeffrey's wounds. The tight cluster, all from the same angle, actually supported Kenneth's version better than a typical stabbing.

Throughout the trial, Jeffrey's family never appeared. Their absence spoke volumes.

Kenneth never testified, but his videotaped confession was played, describing how Jeffrey threw himself onto the knife, how he directed Kenneth to reposition it toward his heart.

The critical moment came with jury instructions. Judge Carol Berkman told jurors that if Kenneth "actively" caused Jeffrey's death, even with consent, it was murder. The defense objected furiously. The law made no distinction between "active" and "passive" participation in assisted suicide.

After five hours of deliberation, the jury returned a verdict: guilty of second-degree murder.

At sentencing on April 4, 2011, Kenneth finally spoke publicly: "Only two people in the world know what happened that night, and one of them is not here no more. I'm no animal, and I ain't got no malice in my heart."

Judge Berkman sentenced him to twenty years to life—but the case was far from over.

Months later, juror Olympia Moy, a Fordham law student, contacted the defense with a sworn affidavit: "If the judge had not instructed us to consider whether Mr. Minor's killing was 'active' or not, I would have voted not guilty to murder." The jury had felt trapped by the judge's interpretation.

On October 7, 2013, the Appellate Division unanimously overturned Kenneth's conviction. The 5-0 ruling found that Judge Berkman's "active/passive" distinction didn't exist in New York law. Her instruction had "mandated a directed verdict of guilt."

Rather than risk acquittal at retrial, prosecutors offered a deal: plead guilty to manslaughter, twelve years total. With time served, Kenneth would be free in seven years.

On October 20, 2014, at his final sentencing, Kenneth showed genuine remorse: "I had the chance to do the right thing, and I didn't. I failed Mr. Locker that night because of my own greed. I'll never let that happen again."

Jeffrey's elaborate plan to save his family through insurance fraud ultimately failed. Federal Judge William Kuntz voided the $4 million Principal Life policy because Jeffrey had lied about his income. Other companies also refused to pay. Of $18 million in policies, the family collected only about $5 million from older policies where suicide exclusions had expired.

The case became known as the "Harlem Kevorkian" case, forcing the justice system to confront impossible questions: Can someone consent to their own murder? When does assisted suicide become homicide?

Kenneth Minor was granted parole in 2019 after serving ten years of his sentence. He had entered prison as a desperate drug addict who'd made the worst decision of his life, and he emerged a decade later into a world that had moved on without him.

CHAPTER 5
THE I-70 RAPIST

The maintenance supervisor backed away from the bedroom doorway, his face draining of color. His scream cut through the morning quiet of the west Wichita apartment complex, a sound that would haunt everyone who heard it.

It was 10:00 a.m. on June 25, 2002. What should have been a simple fix for a beeping smoke detector had become a nightmare.

The apartment manager had summoned him after a resident complained about the intermittent alarm from the vacant unit next door. Smoke still hung in the air as they pushed through the unlocked door, its acrid smell mixing with something else—something metallic and wrong. The carpet showed scorch marks where fires had burned themselves out during the night, but the smoke damage wasn't what sent the maintenance supervisor stumbling backward into the hallway.

In the bedroom, sprawled across the floor in the harsh

morning light, lay the nude body of a woman. Where her head should have been, there was only blood-soaked carpet.

The manager's hands trembled so violently that she could barely dial 911. Her voice cracked as she tried to explain to the dispatcher what they'd found. Within minutes, the peaceful Tuesday morning transformed into something else entirely. Police cruisers filled the parking lot. Yellow tape sectioned off the building. Residents pressed against the perimeter, craning to see, whispering theories to each other about what could have happened in their quiet complex.

Detective John Martin ducked under the tape and approached the scene. Fifteen years of working homicides in Wichita had shown him humanity's capacity for cruelty, but the crime scene photographer intercepted him at the door, his usual professional detachment replaced by something hollow.

"Take a minute before you go in there," the photographer said quietly. "This one's different."

Martin stepped into the apartment and immediately understood. This wasn't just murder; this was rage made manifest.

―――

The apartment bore witness to two distinct stories: savage violence and a desperate, failed attempt to erase it.

Burn patterns scarred the carpet in two places, one near the patio door and another in the corner of the living room. The perpetrator had doused sections with accelerant and set them ablaze, but modern flame-retardant carpet had refused to cooperate with his plan. Instead of consuming the evidence in flames, the carpet had smoldered through the night, filling the apartment with smoke that had triggered the alarm, leading to the discovery.

Crime Scene Investigator Andrew Maul worked methodically through the chaos, cataloging each piece of evidence. The living room yielded a partially smoked Marlboro cigarette, carelessly abandoned. An upside-down CD player. A red bottle cap. A maid's cleaning cart stood near the entrance, abandoned mid-shift. And there, in a dark pool that had soaked deep into the carpet fibers, lay a single human tooth.

The kitchen told its own story. Two sets of keys and seventy-nine cents in loose change sat on the counter, mundane objects that now seemed ominous. An empty Popov vodka bottle rested against the wall near the bedroom entrance, its contents long consumed.

The bathroom made investigators pause. Every surface—floor, sink, vanity, toilet—had been buried under a thick layer of powdered cleanser. The white powder showed distinct drag marks across the floor, as if something heavy and wet had been pulled through it. The killer had dumped an entire container, maybe more, in a frantic attempt to clean up evidence that refused to disappear.

Blood had seeped into places the killer had never thought to clean. Dark stains marked the living room and bedroom carpets, creating a trail of violence through the apartment. A shelf inside the refrigerator bore a crimson smear. Outside, on the small patio, three dark stains marred the wooden railing, their significance not yet understood.

The patio door hung askew, its frame splintered where someone had forced it. The deadbolt mechanism lay on the floor inside, ripped from its housing with enough force to crack the wood around it.

In the bedroom, investigators found a pile of women's clothing, each piece heavy with blood: a t-shirt, jeans with a black belt still threaded through the loops, underwear, and sneakers. The clothes had been removed, not torn off, and left in a heap. Maul carefully bagged each item, and that was when he found it—in the pocket of the jeans, a folded piece of paper with a name and phone number scrawled across it: "Doug."

Dr. Jaime Oeberst arrived to examine the body, his medical bag in hand and his expression grim. What he found exceeded even his worst expectations.

The decapitation hadn't been clean or quick. Multiple cuts, some shallow and hesitant, others deep and forceful, showed where the killer had hacked and sawed through muscle and bone between the third and fourth cervical vertebrae. The varying depths and angles suggested struggle, determination, and most horrifying of all, that some of the cutting had occurred while the victim was still alive, still breathing, and still capable of feeling everything.

The violence visited upon her body defied comprehension. Four stab wounds had punctured the left side of her chest. The killer had driven the knife deep—one thrust penetrating five inches into her heart, another going nearly seven inches, ensuring death several times over. A third wound had collapsed her left lung, filling it with blood. The fourth had traveled through her abdomen with such force that it had pierced her liver, stomach, and even nicked her spine.

Her forearms told the story of her final fight. Defensive wounds, three on her right arm and one on her left, showed where she'd raised her hands against the knife, trying desperately to protect herself. The medical examiner would count sixty-three separate bruises across her arms and legs, each one evidence of the blows rained down during a prolonged beating.

Small puncture wounds dotted her left shoulder and the base of her neck, different from the stabbing injuries. These were deliberate, controlled marks where the tip of a knife had been pressed into skin, breaking it just enough to draw blood. Control wounds. Terror wounds. The killer had used the knife point to keep her still, to make her comply before the final violence began.

What happened after death was perhaps even more disturbing. Two long cuts ran the length of her back, shallow and bloodless, carved into skin that no longer bled. The genital area had been mutilated with intersecting cuts. Knife wounds flanked the anus. A deep stab wound between the vagina and anus had penetrated the vaginal canal. All these injuries showed no vital tissue response—they were inflicted on a corpse, the killer's rage continuing even after life had fled.

The left side of the body showed extensive burns: blistering and charring consistent with accelerant and flame. The killer had poured flammable liquid on the body and set it alight, but like the carpet, the fire had failed to consume the evidence.

By noon, fingerprints had given the body a name: Lucille Gallegos, forty-three years old. A housekeeper who'd worked at the complex for years.

Somewhere in Wichita, her family was about to receive news that would shatter their world.

———

The investigation exploded outward in multiple directions simultaneously. Every detective who could be spared joined the search for Lucille's severed head. They understood the psychology behind taking it—killers removed heads to prevent identification, to keep as trophies, or to dispose of far from the crime scene. Each possibility drove a different search strategy.

Trash collection was halted across western Wichita. Officers in protective gear climbed into dumpsters, sifting through garbage bags in the suffocating summer heat. Others walked the routes garbage trucks had taken that morning, checking every bin and container.

Dive teams assembled at every body of water within a ten-mile radius. They searched retention ponds behind shopping centers, drainage ditches along highways, and the murky depths of the Arkansas River. Cadaver dogs and their handlers swept through vacant lots, construction sites, and the scrubland at the edge of the city.

The search expanded. Highway patrol officers checked rest stops and roadside areas where something could be thrown from a moving vehicle. The theory that the killer might have driven out of the city with the head, disposing of it miles away, meant the search area grew exponentially with each passing hour.

But Lucille's head would never be found.

Investigators began reconstructing Lucille's final day. Security footage from a liquor store half a mile away provided the first solid timeline. At 6:00 p.m. on June 24, the camera captured Lucille purchasing a bottle of Popov vodka, the same brand found empty in the apartment. She counted out exact change, smiled at the clerk, and walked out into what would be her last evening.

Witnesses placed her back at the apartment complex around 8:00 p.m., noticeably intoxicated. One resident remembered seeing her stumbling near the laundry room, using the wall for support. Another saw her sitting on the steps of a vacant unit, the vodka bottle beside her, talking to herself—or perhaps to someone just out of sight.

The obvious first suspect was Chris Branch, Lucille's boyfriend. Their relationship was a matter of police record: domestic disturbance calls, reports of shouting matches that woke neighbors, and at least one incident where Lucille had shown up at the emergency room with bruises she wouldn't explain. When detectives arrived at his construction site that afternoon, Chris was operating a backhoe, unaware that his world was about to implode.

They told him Lucille was missing, watching his reaction carefully. The transformation was immediate and genuine. Chris's legs gave out. He collapsed against the side of the backhoe, sobbing. When they finally told him she was dead, he had an emotional breakdown. His foreman confirmed Chris had clocked in at 6:00 a.m., hours before the body was discovered. Three coworkers verified he'd been there all morning. The timeline didn't work.

But there was still that note in Lucille's pocket. "Doug" and a phone number.

Douglas Belt lived directly across from the crime scene, close enough that he could see the vacant apartment's door from his living room window. At forty years old, Doug drove trucks for a living, a job that not only kept him away for days at a time but also meant he was often home at odd hours. He knew both Lucille and Chris from when they'd all lived in the same building months earlier.

Douglas Belt

Detective Martin knocked on Doug's door that evening, just eight hours after the body was discovered. Doug answered immediately, as if he'd been waiting.

The interview started normally enough. Doug expressed shock about Lucille's death, offering condolences he'd surely pass along to Chris when he saw him. But then, without prompting, Doug launched into a detailed account of the previous evening. The information poured out of him.

Chris had come by around 7:00 p.m., Doug said, looking for Lucille. They'd shared a beer and tried to set up Doug's new cell phone, spending maybe thirty minutes together before Chris mentioned going fishing. Doug emphasized how he tried to keep his distance from the couple. They were alcoholics, he explained. Chris got violent when he drank, and Lucille could be nasty, showing up at his door at all hours begging for beer or vodka.

He told a story about intervening months ago when Chris was beating Lucille in Doug's own apartment, positioning himself as the concerned neighbor who'd tried to help. He suggested Lucille had probably spent the night in the vacant unit—she did that sometimes when she was too drunk to go home, he said. The last time he'd seen her, she was stumbling around outside, barely able to walk.

Martin took notes, nodded, and thanked Doug for his time. However, something about the conversation felt rehearsed, as if Doug had been practicing his lines.

For three months, the investigation ground forward. The DNA laboratory worked methodically through the evidence. Blood from the patio railing. Samples from under Lucille's fingernails. The cigarette butt. Every surface that might hold genetic material.

The results, when they came, provided both answers and frustration. The blood on the patio railing contained two DNA profiles mixed together: Lucille's and an unknown male's. The killer had been injured during the attack, his blood mixing with his victim's. Chris Branch's DNA was tested immediately, but it didn't match. The boyfriend was excluded definitively.

But without a suspect to compare it to, the unknown male DNA was just a string of genetic markers waiting for a name.

Detectives interviewed every resident of the complex, some multiple times. They tracked down former residents who'd moved away. They questioned delivery drivers, maintenance workers—anyone who might have had reason to be in that apartment. They pulled Lucille's phone records, examined her bank statements, and interviewed coworkers and family members about potential enemies or threats.

The investigation consumed thousands of hours. Detectives followed leads that went nowhere, chased theories that dissolved under scrutiny. The DNA evidence mocked them—proof of the killer's identity that meant nothing without a match.

———

November 8, 2002, started like any other day. By noon, it would change everything.

Doug Belt walked into a Payless ShoeSource in east Wichita carrying what looked like a handgun. He demanded money, waving the weapon at terrified employees. The robbery was bold, desperate, and ultimately doomed. As Doug fled with the cash, employees called 911 with his description and license plate number.

The chase was brief but dramatic. Doug's white sedan weaved through traffic as patrol cars converged from multiple directions. Officers watched him throw objects from the driver's window—the stolen money, the receipt, and finally the gun itself, which bounced off the pavement and skittered into a ditch.

When they finally boxed him in at a red light, Doug didn't resist. The gun turned out to be a BB pistol, realistic enough to terrify but incapable of the damage he'd threatened. He was arrested, processed, and locked in a holding cell to await arraignment.

At the homicide division, word of Doug Belt's arrest reached Detective Martin within hours. The name triggered immediate recognition—the helpful neighbor from the Gallegos crime scene, the one who'd volunteered so much information without being asked. Martin pulled the case file, found the note from Lucille's pocket with "Doug" written on it, and felt the pieces clicking together in his mind.

They needed Doug's DNA, but they needed it legally. The warrant was carefully crafted; they would collect DNA to compare to evidence on the BB gun Doug had touched during the robbery. No mention of the Gallegos case. No hint of their real purpose.

Doug submitted to the cheek swab without protest, even joking with the technician about how many crime shows featured DNA evidence these days. The sample was hand-delivered to the laboratory with a priority rush order.

The wait stretched across three agonizing days. When the phone finally rang, the lab technician's voice was tight with excitement. It was a match. The probability of the DNA belonging to anyone other than Douglas Belt was one in 158 million. His blood was on that patio railing, mixed with Lucille's, placing him at the scene during the violence.

November 9, 2002. Interview Room 3 at the Wichita Police Department. Doug Belt sat across from Detective Martin, the metal table between them reflecting the harsh fluorescent lights. Martin read Doug his rights slowly, clearly. Doug waived them with a casual gesture, still playing the helpful citizen.

When Martin laid out the DNA evidence and watched Doug's face change as he explained what it meant, the façade cracked. Doug's story shifted.

Douglas Belt admitted he had been with Lucille that night, but it wasn't what they thought. It was consensual and mutual. After Chris had left his apartment, Doug had walked over to check on Lucille, bringing a fresh bottle of vodka to share. She was drunk but happy to see him, and she'd invited him in. They'd sat on the living room floor, drinking and talking about their problems.

One thing had led to another, Doug claimed. They'd started kissing and moved to the bedroom. Things had gotten heated, but they never went all the way. He admitted to touching her intimately but insisted she'd stopped him before actual intercourse, placing her hand on his chest and saying it wasn't right because of Chris. Doug claimed he'd immediately agreed, and mentioned he had a girlfriend anyway.

Then someone had knocked on the door. Doug had assumed it was Chris looking for Lucille. She'd panicked and told Doug to leave through the patio door. He'd done exactly that —went out back, grabbed the railing to vault over it, and jogged back to his apartment. The last time he saw Lucille, he said, she was alive, unharmed, and walking him to the patio door.

The only injury he'd sustained was a small cut on his palm, probably from vaulting the railing. That explained his blood outside, he suggested. A tiny cut, a transfer of blood to the railing, nothing more.

Martin let the silence stretch before responding. He explained what the crime scene had revealed—that Doug's blood and Lucille's blood were mixed together, wet simultaneously, which only happened if both were actively bleeding during contact. That meant violence, struggle—both of them injured at the same moment.

Doug's explanations grew increasingly desperate. Maybe Lucille had been on her period? Maybe she'd cut herself earlier? Maybe someone else had come in after he'd left? When Martin pressed harder, laying out photo after photo of the crime scene, the devastation visited upon Lucille's body, Doug's jaw clenched.

"I want a lawyer. We're done."

Doug's arrest for murder triggered something unexpected in the KBI's cold case unit. Senior Special Agent Ronald Hagen remembered the name from over a decade ago. In 1991, Douglas Belt had been a suspect in a series of rapes along the I-70 corridor. Hagen pulled the old files, dusty boxes that contained horrors from another era.

Between 1989 and 1994, a predator had terrorized women across Kansas. Seven confirmed attacks followed an identical pattern that spoke to a methodical, evolving predator. The rapist struck between midnight and 3:00 a.m., choosing women who lived alone. He broke in through windows or jimmied doors, brought duct tape and a knife, and spent hours destroying his victims' sense of safety.

The first victim, identified in records only as A.H., had been washing her hair in the shower on March 25, 1989, when hands had grabbed her from behind. The attacker had wrapped tape around her eyes before she could see his face, bound her wrists behind her back, and subjected her to repeated sexual assaults. He'd left her tied on the bathroom floor, where she wasn't found until morning.

Each subsequent attack grew bolder. The September 1989 victim remembered the knife pressed against her throat as her attacker whispered, "Maybe I should just slash your throat and get it over with." Another woman recalled him forcing her to shower afterward while he watched, then making her lie still while he arranged her body in different positions, as if setting up a scene.

The victims described similar details: a tall man, strong enough to overpower them quickly, who seemed to know their routines. He took small trophies—thirty-eight dollars from one victim's purse, a hundred from another, pieces of jewelry that held sentimental rather than monetary value. However, the attacks stopped abruptly in 1994.

In March 1991, Doug Belt had volunteered to give blood for DNA testing when investigators had canvassed men in McPherson County. The lab tech drew his blood, labeled the vial, and sent it for processing. Unfortunately, somewhere in the chain of custody, a catastrophic error occurred. Another person's DNA was labeled with Doug's name, while Doug's actual sample was marked "unknown." When the FBI tested what they believed was Doug's sample, it didn't match the rapist's DNA. Doug was cleared and removed from the suspect list.

Now, eleven years later, Agent Hagen ordered a new DNA comparison. Doug's fresh sample was tested against the old rape kit evidence, preserved all these years in freezers, waiting for technology and opportunity to converge.

The matches came back one by one. March 1989: positive match. September 1989: positive match. Every single rape in the series matched Douglas Belt's DNA profile. The I-70 Rapist had been identified at last, but the statute of limitations had long since expired for the rapes. He would never stand trial for those seven women's suffering.

KBI Director Larry Welch held a press conference, his voice heavy with regret as he admitted the agency's failure. The mislabeled DNA had allowed a serial rapist to remain free for over a decade, during which time he'd escalated to murder. Welch apologized to the victims, to Lucille Gallegos's family, and to the community that had been failed by the very system meant to protect them.

In October 2004, the Sedgwick County Courthouse was filled with reporters, family members, and survivors of Doug's previous attacks. Prosecutors Marc Bennett and Barry Disney laid out their case. They had DNA evidence, the note in Lucille's pocket, Doug's changing stories, and now, under Kansas law, they could present evidence of his prior crimes.

One by one, six women took the stand to describe their attacks from years past. Their voices wavered but didn't break as they recounted the duct tape, the knife, and the hours of terror. Some had never spoken publicly about their assaults. Now they faced their attacker across a courtroom, their testimony painting a picture of a predator who had evolved from rapist to killer.

The defense tried to redirect blame toward Chris Branch, but the strategy collapsed against the forensic evidence. Chris's DNA wasn't at the scene. Doug's was everywhere—in blood on the railing, on the cigarette, in the very fabric of the crime.

Doug never took the stand. His silence spoke volumes.

After two weeks of testimony, the jury deliberated for just three hours. Guilty of capital murder. Guilty of attempted rape. Guilty of aggravated arson. During the penalty phase, they found that the crime had been committed to avoid arrest and was especially heinous and cruel. Their recommendation was unanimous: death.

On November 17, 2004, Judge Rebecca Pilshaw formally sentenced Douglas Belt to death by lethal injection. Doug stood silent, offering no apology, no explanation, and no revelation about what he'd done with Lucille's head.

———

For over a decade, Douglas Belt sat in a cell at El Dorado Correctional Facility, filing appeals that went nowhere and maintaining an innocence that no one believed. He gave no interviews, wrote no confessions, provided no closure to the families desperate for answers.

On April 13, 2016, guards found him unresponsive during a routine check. Prison medical staff worked to revive him, but at 3:00 p.m., Douglas Stephen Belt was pronounced dead.

Natural causes, the coroner determined. His health had been declining for months. He was fifty-four years old.

Lucille's daughter, April, learned of his death from a reporter calling for comment. She felt shock, then relief, then a crushing return of grief. The appeals were over, but so was any hope of learning where her mother's remains were hidden. The family had chosen forgiveness not for Doug but for themselves, to avoid becoming his final victims.

The Belt case transformed how Kansas handles DNA evidence, spurring new protocols and safeguards that remain in place today. The vacant apartment where Lucille died was cleaned, repainted, and rented to new tenants who knew nothing of its history. However, for the investigators who worked the case, the six women who survived Doug's earlier attacks, and Lucille's family, the scars remain. Douglas Belt died, taking his secrets with him—the location of Lucille's head, his true motivations, and perhaps other victims never connected to him. What survived him was the evidence of his cruelty, the testimony of his victims, and the certainty that the I-70 Rapist would never hurt anyone again.

CHAPTER 6
THE PERFECT MURDER

September 8, 2013. The date should have meant something different entirely.

Two mushroom foragers pushed through the morning mist in Kreuther Forest, their wicker baskets empty, their hopes high for chanterelles after the recent rains. The woods north of Regensburg stretched endlessly, a maze of pine and beech where locals had hunted fungi for generations. Thirty kilometers from the medieval city center, where the Danube River curves through Bavaria's heart, these woods held secrets beneath every fallen log.

The older forager, a man who'd walked these paths since childhood, noticed something white protruding from the earth near a cluster of moss-covered stones. Not the cream color of a prized Steinpilz mushroom. Something else. Something wrong.

Bone.

He used his walking stick to push aside the leaves to reveal more bones scattered across the forest floor—some partially buried, others lying exposed like broken porcelain against the dark soil. The skull fragment was unmistakable. However, it was the strange white substance coating everything that made his blood run cold. The powder had hardened into crystalline chunks, fused with the remains like volcanic ash turned to stone.

Within an hour, the Bavarian State Police had sealed off a perimeter that stretched fifty meters in every direction. The forensic team arrived from Munich in unmarked vans, their equipment cases containing tools for the worst kinds of puzzles. The lead investigator stood at the edge of what appeared to be a shallow grave, studying the scene with practiced detachment that couldn't quite hide his revulsion.

The remains weren't just buried; they'd been chemically destroyed. The white substance appeared to be quicklime—calcium oxide, a caustic chemical that generates extreme heat of up to 470° Celsius when mixed with water. The reaction creates a highly alkaline environment that dissolves soft tissue and degrades even bones. Someone had tried to erase a human being from existence through chemistry.

The forensic anthropologist worked through the afternoon, photographing each fragment before sealing it in evidence bags. The chemical treatment had devastated the body—soft tissue completely dissolved, bones showing severe degradation, and some portions reduced to a soap-like substance through a process called saponification. Scraps of fabric, possibly women's undergarments, had fused with the mineralized remains.

Four strands of hair clung to a hardened clump of the lime mixture—a miracle of preservation that would prove more important than anyone could imagine.

Near the grave's edge, investigators discovered a spade partly buried under autumn leaves from the previous year. It looked relatively new, the price sticker still partially visible despite months of exposure. A common brand that was sold at hardware stores throughout Bavaria.

The remains were transported to the Institute of Legal Medicine in Munich. Initial examination suggested a female victim based on pelvic bone structure, but the extensive chemical damage made immediate identification nearly impossible. The team would need advanced DNA analysis, comparing genetic markers from the bones to missing persons in their database.

In Regensburg, investigators pulled files on every woman who'd vanished in the region over the past five years. One name kept surfacing: Maria Baumer, twenty-six years old, missing since May 2012. The young woman who'd supposedly left to walk the Camino de Santiago, whose fiancé had appeared on national television begging for her return.

Sixteen months after her disappearance, on what would have been her wedding day, Maria Baumer had finally been found.

―――

Regensburg in 2012 was a city suspended between centuries. Medieval towers cast shadows over biotechnology firms, and UNESCO World Heritage sites shared streets with wind energy companies. The Danube flowed through it all, carrying cargo barges past thousand-year-old bridges where university students gathered to drink beer in the sunset.

Maria Baumer belonged to both worlds—the traditional and the progressive. She stood at nearly six feet tall, with an athlete's build from years of hiking the Bavarian Alps with the Catholic Rural Youth Movement. Her faith wasn't just Sunday observance; it was woven into everything she did. The silver cross necklace she never removed had been a confirmation gift from her grandmother.

Her path to success hadn't been straightforward. The geoecology program at the University of Bayreuth was notoriously difficult—an interdisciplinary maze of chemistry, biology, geology, and environmental science. Maria had struggled initially, spending entire nights in the library, surviving on coffee and determination. However, her thesis on soil remediation techniques for contaminated industrial sites had earned the highest honors. Her professor had called it "groundbreaking work that could reshape how we approach environmental restoration."

By May 2012, everything was falling into place. She'd beaten out forty candidates for a position as a wind turbine technician with one of Germany's leading renewable energy companies. The job combined her environmental passion with practical application—climbing massive turbines to conduct maintenance, analyzing performance data, and contributing to Germany's Energiewende. Her first week on the job, she'd sent her twin sister, Barbara, a photo from atop a 100-meter turbine, the Bavarian countryside spreading endlessly below.

Six days before she vanished, Maria had achieved another dream: election as state chairwoman of the Catholic Rural Youth Movement Bavaria. The position would let her shape programs for thousands of young Catholics across the state. She'd prepared for months, developing initiatives that bridged traditional faith with modern environmental stewardship. Her acceptance speech had brought a standing ovation.

Finally, it was her relationship with Christian F. that seemed to complete the picture of a perfect life.

Christian had entered Maria's life in January 2008, when grief had made her vulnerable. Her close friend Beni had died in an accident—a death for which Maria somehow blamed herself, though she never explained why. She'd been drowning in guilt when Christian had appeared at a church youth group meeting, quiet and attentive, offering comfort without demanding anything in return.

He seemed ideal: a psychiatric nurse at Bezirkskrankenhaus Regensburg, one of Bavaria's most prestigious mental health facilities. He'd graduated from the elite Domspatzen-Gymnasium, the cathedral school famous for its boys' choir. He spoke of medical school with confidence, describing future plans to specialize in psychiatry. His family owned a riding stable in Bernhardswald—solid, respectable people with deep roots in the community.

Their long-distance relationship had lasted until late 2011, when Maria moved into Christian's Regensburg apartment. The space reflected his medical ambitions—anatomy textbooks stacked on shelves, medical journals scattered across the coffee table, a desktop computer where he studied for exams late into the night.

But behind the façade of medical ambition lay darker secrets. Christian had been sexually abusing teenage boys from the Domspatzen choir school, crimes that had gone undetected while he maintained his image as a respectable healthcare worker and devoted partner.

Christian F.

His medical studies were another elaborate fiction. He'd been failing exams for years, each failure hidden behind increasingly complex lies. To Maria, he was always just one test away from advancement. To his parents, he was excelling but modest about his achievements. The truth was that Christian had neither the ability nor the genuine desire to become a doctor. The textbooks were props in a performance he couldn't sustain.

Everything changed in April 2012, when Valerie S. arrived at his psychiatric ward.

―――

Valerie was a young woman in her mid-twenties who had been treated for severe depression at Bezirkskrankenhaus

Regensburg. Childhood trauma had left her fragile, seeking help for wounds that went deeper than anyone initially realized. She was exactly the kind of vulnerable patient that psychiatric facilities are meant to protect.

Christian was assigned to her care team—a trusted position that gave him access to her medical files, her daily routine, and her deepest vulnerabilities revealed through therapy sessions. He began visiting her room more frequently than protocol required, bringing small gifts—chocolate, magazines, books he thought she'd enjoy. To other staff, he appeared to be a caring nurse going above and beyond. To Valerie, confused and medicated, he seemed like the only person who truly understood her pain.

The boundaries eroded gradually. First, he gave her his personal phone number in case she needed to talk. Then came the friend request on Facebook under a false name, claiming to be an American patient who'd been through similar struggles. Through this fake persona, he extracted information about her fears, her dreams, and her favorite music. By early May 2012, Christian had conducted over 200 pages worth of internet searches about Valerie and her family in a single day.

He brought her medical file home, a violation that could have ended his career. Late at night, while Maria slept in their bed, Christian studied Valerie's psychiatric evaluations, her medication regimen, and the transcript of her therapy sessions. He was learning her from the inside out, the way a scientist might study a specimen.

By May 10, Christian's correspondence with Valerie under his American pseudonym was feeding a growing obsession. However, he couldn't act on his desires while Maria existed. The engagement, the wedding planned for September, the entire life he'd constructed—it all stood between him and his new fixation.

A normal person might have ended the engagement, but Christian had spent his entire adult life constructing elaborate deceptions. The thought of admitting failure—that his medical studies were a sham, that he wanted to pursue a teenage psychiatric patient—would destroy the image he'd cultivated. In his mind, shaped by narcissistic pathology that psychiatrists would later document, there was only one solution that preserved his façade while creating the freedom he craved.

Maria had to disappear.

Christian's position at the psychiatric hospital provided access to restricted medications. Lorazepam, marketed as Tavor in Germany, was a powerful benzodiazepine used for severe anxiety. Tramadol, a synthetic opioid, was used to treat chronic pain. Together, they created a potentially lethal combination. The benzodiazepine would induce deep sedation while the opioid suppressed respiratory function. The victim would simply stop breathing.

On May 22, Christian made a purchase at a Regensburg hardware store. Using Maria's debit card, he bought a spade. The same day, he acquired quicklime and anhydrite binder from a construction supply company. His medical training had taught him that quicklime, when mixed with moisture, creates temperatures exceeding 840 degrees Fahrenheit while generating a caustic alkaline solution. It was chemistry weaponized for concealment.

The burial site had been selected in advance: a remote section of Kreuther Forest near Bernhardswald, where he'd played as a child. He knew which paths the hikers used, which areas the hunters avoided. The spot he chose was accessible by car but invisible from any trail, surrounded by dense undergrowth that would conceal fresh digging.

Maria, meanwhile, was planning their wedding with characteristic attention to detail. 250 wedding invitations sat in cream-colored boxes in their apartment, addressed and stamped, waiting to be mailed on Saturday, May 26. She'd chosen the readings for the ceremony, confirmed the flower arrangements, and finalized the seating chart that carefully balanced both families' social dynamics.

On Thursday, May 24, she sent her sister a text message filled with emoji hearts, excited about the upcoming weekend. She'd finally have time to mail the invitations, finish the last details, and maybe go riding at Christian's family stable. Her new job was challenging but fulfilling. Her position with the Catholic Youth Movement would be announced in the church bulletin on Sunday.

Sadly, she had less than forty-eight hours to live.

―――――

Friday, May 25, 2012, began like any other. Maria left for work at 7:00 a.m., kissing Christian goodbye at the apartment door. She spent the day at the wind farm, climbing turbines, analyzing performance data, and discussing grid integration challenges with the engineering team. Her colleagues would later describe her as particularly cheerful that day, talking about the wedding and inviting them to the reception.

The barbecue at Christian's family riding stable in Bernhardswald started at 7:00 p.m. Maria arrived straight from work, still wearing her company polo shirt, her hair pulled back in the practical ponytail she favored for climbing turbines. She helped Christian's mother prepare salads in the kitchen, discussing plans for the rehearsal dinner while slicing vegetables.

The evening unfolded with the comfortable rhythm of family gatherings. Maria rode horses with Christian's sister-in-law as the sun set over the Bavarian countryside, their laughter carrying across the fields. Christian manned the grill, accepting compliments on his marinade recipe, playing the role of devoted fiancé to perfection. No one noticed that he checked his phone obsessively, or that his smile never quite reached his eyes.

They left around 11:30 p.m., Maria drowsy from the wine. The drive back to Regensburg took twenty minutes through dark country roads. Christian drove while Maria dozed in the passenger seat, her hand resting on his knee in unconscious intimacy. The wedding invitations waited in their apartment like promises about to be broken.

Once home, Maria headed straight to the bedroom while Christian went to the kitchen. He often made her hot chocolate before bed—Swiss Miss with extra marshmallows, a childhood comfort she'd never outgrown. Tonight, he prepared it with special care, stirring until the powder dissolved completely, making sure the temperature was just right.

The Lorazepam and Tramadol dissolved easily, tasteless in the sweet drink.

Maria was already in bed, checking her phone one last time, when Christian brought the mug. She smiled, sitting up to accept it and taking a long sip immediately. "Perfect," she said —a word that would echo with terrible irony. They talked about tomorrow's plans while she drank—mailing invitations in the morning, maybe visiting the church to finalize ceremony details.

Within fifteen minutes, Maria's words began to slur. The room was spinning, she said. Maybe she'd had too much wine at the barbecue. Christian helped her lie down, pulled the covers up to her chin, and told her to rest. Her last conscious thought, perhaps, was gratitude for his care.

The drugs worked exactly as his research had indicated. First came the deep sedation from the Lorazepam, her consciousness dissolving. Then the Tramadol began its work, depressing her respiratory system, each breath becoming shallower and less frequent. Christian sat beside her, watching and waiting. At some point between 2:00 a.m. and 8:00 a.m. Maria Baumer's breathing stopped entirely.

Whether Christian took additional action to ensure her death—suffocation, strangulation—would remain a question for the courts. What was certain was that by sunrise on Saturday, May 26, 2012, Maria was dead in the bed they'd shared, while 250 wedding invitations sat unmailed in their cream-colored boxes.

———

Christian worked quickly in the early morning darkness. Maria's body was already stiffening—he had only hours before rigor mortis would make moving her impossible. He pulled sheets from their linen closet, the ones with the delicate embroidery they'd received as an engagement gift from her aunt. The fabric that had once covered them both in sleep now became a shroud. He lifted her body, heavier now in death than she'd ever seemed in life, and navigated the apartment's narrow hallway. Outside, he loaded Maria into his car trunk, closing it with a soft click.

The drive to Kreuther Forest took less than thirty minutes. The burial site he'd selected was exactly as he'd planned—secluded, accessible, invisible. The grave didn't need to be deep; the chemicals would do the real work.

He arranged Maria's body in the shallow depression, then poured the quicklime and anhydrite mixture over her remains. The powder covered her like snow, white and innocent-looking, belying its destructive purpose. When moisture activated it, the chemical reaction he'd researched would do its work, destroying evidence through extreme heat and caustic conditions. In his haste to leave, the spade slipped from his grasp, falling near the grave's edge. He'd retrieve it later, he thought, but later never came.

Back at the apartment, Christian began constructing his narrative. At 9:00 a.m., he left for his supposed morning jog —a detail neighbors might remember. When he returned an hour later, he began making phone calls. First to her sister Barbara: Maria wasn't home; had she heard from her? Then to Maria's parents: Strange, she'd left her phone and engagement ring but taken nothing else.

The lie evolved over the next three days. He claimed Maria had called him twice—once from Nuremberg, once from Hamburg. She sounded stressed, needed time to think, and mentioned walking the Camino de Santiago, a centuries-old pilgrimage route across Spain. The calls never existed, but phone records wouldn't be checked for weeks.

He accessed Maria's Facebook account, sending himself a message: "My darling, it hurts. Forgive me, but I can't do otherwise." The cryptic note suggested emotional turmoil, perhaps suicidal ideation—seeds of misdirection planted for investigators to find.

On Tuesday, May 29, three days after the murder, Christian finally filed a missing person report. He presented himself as confused and hurt but hopeful. She'd been stressed about the wedding, he explained, overwhelmed by her new responsibilities. Sometimes people just needed space.

Summer 2012 saw Christian transform into Regensburg's most sympathetic figure. The abandoned fiancé who couldn't bear to mail the wedding invitations. The devoted partner who organized search parties every weekend. The grieving man who kept Maria's belongings exactly as she'd left them, her coffee cup still on the kitchen counter.

The Catholic Rural Youth Movement mobilized hundreds of volunteers. They spread across Bavaria with flyers bearing Maria's photograph—her warm smile, her distinctive height mentioned prominently. Christian often led these searches, comforting other volunteers when hope flagged, maintaining Facebook pages dedicated to finding her.

He told people that Maria's disappearance had forced him to abandon his medical studies. The tragedy had broken his concentration, made it impossible to focus on exams. This generated enormous sympathy while conveniently explaining his academic failure—a failure that had actually occurred years before Maria's death.

The deception reached its pinnacle on November 28, 2012, when Christian appeared on "Aktenzeichen XY... ungelöst" alongside Maria's mother, Barbara Baumer. Germany's most-watched crime program had featured missing persons cases for decades, its appeals reaching millions of viewers.

In the television studio, Christian sat composed while Barbara wept openly. He produced Maria's phone and engagement ring as props, explaining how she'd left them behind. His voice caught at just the right moments, his hand reaching out to comfort Barbara.

The program included footage filmed at a Regensburg church. Christian lit candles before a statue of the Virgin Mary, his lips moving in apparent prayer. "I try to send her strength through my prayers," he told the camera. "I wish she would contact us." The image of the grieving fiancé seeking solace in faith moved viewers across Germany.

Host Rudi Cerne, a veteran of hundreds of cases, was completely convinced. Christian's performance generated nationwide sympathy and hundreds of tips—supposed sightings on the Jakobsweg, in Berlin, in Munich. Each false lead was investigated while Maria's remains lay decomposing in the forest just thirty kilometers from where Christian played his role.

September 8, 2013—the date Maria and Christian should have celebrated their first wedding anniversary—brought the discovery that changed everything. When DNA analysis confirmed the remains belonged to Maria Baumer, the investigation transformed overnight from a missing person case to a homicide.

Investigators quickly dismantled Christian's story. Phone records proved the calls from Maria never existed. The spade at the grave site was traced to the hardware store purchase made with Maria's debit card.

Under interrogation, Christian's story shifted. He now claimed Maria had accidentally overdosed on medication he'd illegally obtained for her anxiety and pain. Panicking about the consequences, he'd hidden her body. It was a "stupid accident" and nothing more.

But investigators weren't convinced. The quicklime, the premeditation evident in the spade purchase, the elaborate cover-up—none of it suggested panic. It suggested planning.

Still, without definitive proof of murder rather than accidental death, prosecutors faced a challenge. The chemical destruction of the remains made determining the exact cause of death impossible. Initial toxicology tests on the degraded bones found no drug traces. In November 2013, Christian was released from custody.

———

Free again, Christian couldn't resist returning to his obsession. In April 2014, he finally acted on the fantasies that had arguably motivated Maria's murder. He pursued Valerie S. relentlessly—hundreds of messages, unexpected visits, constant pressure disguised as concern.

When Valerie finally agreed to meet him at her apartment for tea, Christian saw his opportunity. He slipped Lorazepam into her drink. Valerie felt the drowsiness immediately but managed to resist his advances and eventually cut off all contact. Blood tests confirmed the presence of the drug, and Christian was arrested.

Christian's 2016 trial exposed the full scope of his predatory behavior. Beyond drugging Valerie with Lorazepam, the same sedative that would eventually be found in Maria's remains, he was convicted of sexually abusing two underage boys from the Domspatzen choir school where he'd once been a student himself.

The court-ordered psychiatric evaluation painted a chilling portrait: Christian was diagnosed as a conflict-averse narcissist with pedophilic tendencies. He systematically targeted vulnerable individuals, including depressed patients, troubled teenagers, and anyone whose trust he could exploit. The psychiatrist noted that Christian used his medical knowledge like a weapon, deploying drugs to incapacitate victims who trusted him. He viewed other people not as human beings but as objects to manipulate for his own gratification.

This pattern of drugging, exploitation of trust, and targeting of the vulnerable cast Maria's death in an even darker light. She hadn't just been murdered; she'd been the victim of a serial predator who had been perfecting his methods for years.

Yet even this wasn't enough to retry him for Maria's murder, and the case went cold again.

Maria's family refused to give up. Their formal complaints to higher prosecutors in 2019 coincided with revolutionary advances in forensic toxicology. New mass spectrometry techniques could detect drug traces at concentrations fifty times smaller than previously possible.

When the investigation team applied these techniques to preserved evidence, they found what earlier tests had missed: definitive traces of Lorazepam and Tramadol in Maria's hair and bone marrow. The drugs were embedded in the hair shaft itself, proving they'd been in her system when that hair was growing—impossible if she'd taken them voluntarily just once.

Forensic IT specialists, using recovery techniques that hadn't existed in 2013, also uncovered Christian's deleted search history:

"der perfekte mord" — the perfect murder

"perfektes mordgift" — perfect murder poison

"Mord mit Gift" — murder with poison

"Lorazepam letale dosis" — lethal dose of Lorazepam

"Tramadol Überdosis Symptome" — Tramadol overdose symptoms

"Guillotine-Griff" — guillotine chokehold

"Körper auflösen Chemikalien" — chemicals to dissolve bodies

The queries painted a picture of premeditation that was impossible to refute.

On December 10, 2019, police arrested Christian for the

second time. This time, prosecutors were confident they had enough to convict.

―――――

The trial began July 1, 2020, at the Landgericht Regensburg. The baroque courthouse, built in the 16th century, had seen countless trials, but rarely one that attracted such attention. Lines formed hours before each session, with media from across Germany competing for the twenty reserved press seats.

Over eighteen trial days, the evidence mounted. The drug traces that proved poisoning. The internet searches that proved premeditation. The pattern established by his attack on Valerie. The DNA evidence that placed him at the grave.

The most devastating moment came when prosecutors played the "Aktenzeichen XY" footage. The courtroom watched Christian's 2012 performance—the grieving fiancé lighting candles while Maria lay dead in the forest. Several of Maria's family members had to leave the room.

On August 24, 2020, Christian made a partial confession through his lawyers. He admitted to burying Maria's body but maintained her death was accidental. The court wasn't persuaded.

―――――

October 6, 2020, brought the verdict: guilty of murder with particular severity of guilt. Life imprisonment with no possibility of parole for at least twenty years.

Judge Dr. Michael Hammer's words carried the weight of justice delayed but not denied:

"The defendant exploited the complete trust of his victim. He researched methods, acquired materials, and executed his plan while maintaining a facade of normalcy. This was murder of the most treacherous kind."

Christian showed emotion for the first time, his composed mask finally cracking as the reality of life imprisonment registered. In the gallery, Maria's family wept—for their loss, for the years of deception, but also for the relief of finally having answers.

The Federal Court of Justice rejected Christian's appeal on June 9, 2021, making his life sentence final. Christian F., now thirty-seven, remains in a German prison. This is where he will likely stay for decades. In accordance with German privacy laws, only his first name and last initial have been publicly disclosed.

The case changed "Aktenzeichen XY" forever—new protocols now verify the backgrounds of those who appear on the program. Host Rudi Cerne later admitted the revelation "went under his skin" in a way no other case had.

Maria Baumer is buried in a proper grave now, her remains recovered from the forest and given the dignity denied her in death. The cross necklace she always wore was never found, destroyed by the chemicals meant to erase her existence.

CHAPTER 7
THE BIRTHDAY SURPRISE

The silver Dodge Stratus sat alone on the shoulder of Ortega Highway, its engine rumbling into the November darkness while its headlights illuminated nothing but the empty asphalt ahead. At 10:30 p.m. on November 20, 1999, a security guard from Rancho Mission Viejo was making his routine patrol through the isolated mountain pass when something about the abandoned vehicle caused him to slow down. Perhaps it was the way the car sat perfectly still despite the running engine, or how the headlights aimed into the void of the canyon below.

He pulled over to check if someone needed help, thinking perhaps a driver had wandered off to find cell phone reception in this dead zone of Southern California wilderness. As his own headlights swept across the Dodge, thousands of glass fragments glittered on the asphalt beneath the driver's side door. The window had been completely destroyed, not cracked or broken but obliterated. Through the gaping hole where glass should have been, the interior dome light revealed two figures sitting motionless in the front seats.

The security guard approached slowly, calling out to ask if everyone was alright. No response came from inside the vehicle. As he drew closer, the scene inside the car became horrifyingly clear. The man behind the wheel sat at an unnatural angle, his white dress shirt transformed into a canvas of dark stains that spread across his chest and collar. The woman in the passenger seat had slumped forward against the dashboard, and one of her legs extended out through the partially open door, as if she had tried to escape but never made it.

Blood had sprayed across the windshield in a pattern that told its own violent story, and amid the carnage, a small fragment of human bone rested on the dashboard like evidence of the brutality that had occurred here. The guard stumbled backward and radioed for help, his voice shaking as he reported what he'd found on this desolate stretch of highway that locals knew as a dumping ground for secrets.

Orange County Sheriff's deputies transformed the quiet mountain road into a crime scene within minutes of the call. The victims carried identification that revealed them as Dr. Kenneth Stahl, a fifty-seven-year-old anesthesiologist from the affluent coastal community of Huntington Beach, and his wife, Dr. Carolyn Oppy-Stahl, a forty-four-year-old optometrist with a successful practice in Long Beach. His wallet remained in his pocket with credit cards and cash intact, and her purse sat on the floor completely untouched, its contents undisturbed despite the violence that had occurred just inches away.

―――

The lead detective examined the vehicle as forensic teams began their meticulous documentation of every blood drop, every bullet hole, and every shard of glass. The violence exhibited here went far beyond what was necessary to kill two people trapped in a car. At least ten shots had been fired at close range, possibly more, and the absence of shell casings on the ground indicated the killer had used a revolver rather than a semiautomatic weapon. The shooter had stood within arm's reach of the victims, close enough to ensure accuracy. Close enough to see their faces as they died.

A trail of blood drops led from the passenger door across the asphalt, and a woman's shoe lay several feet from the vehicle, suggesting Carolyn had managed to get partway out of the car during the attack before being shot again. The pattern of wounds and blood evidence painted a picture of someone who had tried desperately to escape, who had almost made it to freedom before the killer reloaded and finished what they'd started.

Kenneth still wore his seatbelt, his body held upright by the restraint even in death. One bullet had entered behind his ear and exited through his eye, destroying his glasses and leaving fragments embedded in the headrest. Another had torn through his chest with such force that it had shredded his aorta, causing massive internal bleeding that would have killed him within seconds. His hands remained near the steering wheel, suggesting he hadn't had time to react or defend himself.

Investigators walked the perimeter of the scene, searching for any evidence the killer might have left behind. This particular stretch of Ortega Highway, approximately two miles east of Caspers Wilderness Park, was well known to law enforcement for all the wrong reasons. Drug dealers used these remote miles to conduct business away from prying eyes, gang members disposed of weapons in the surrounding canyons, and more than one body had been discovered dumped along the shoulder over the years. But this wasn't a body dump—this was where the murders had actually occurred.

"Why here?" one detective asked his partner as they studied the positioning of the car. "They live in Huntington Beach, and this road leads away from there, not toward it."

The car had been parked near an emergency call box, one of the few signs of civilization on this lonely stretch of asphalt. If the couple had stopped because of car trouble, they never made it the few feet to the phone. The location felt deliberate, chosen specifically for its isolation and lack of witnesses.

The medical examiner arrived and confirmed that both victims had been dead for approximately ninety minutes when discovered, placing the time of death around 9:00 p.m. The remote location meant no witnesses had heard the shots, no security cameras had captured the killer's arrival or departure, and no passing motorists had seen anything suspicious until the security guard's discovery.

The next morning, investigators began the painstaking process of reconstructing Kenneth and Carolyn Stahl's final day. They had celebrated her forty-fourth birthday with dinner at a Mexican restaurant in Mission Viejo, where the waitress remembered them as a pleasant couple who had seemed to be enjoying their special evening. Carolyn had appeared happy and relaxed, ordering her favorite meal and sharing dessert with her husband.

Earlier that day, Carolyn had spoken to her mother by phone, mentioning that Kenneth had promised her a birthday surprise that evening. The investigation revealed that the route from the restaurant to their Huntington Beach home would have taken them north on Interstate 5, a straight shot up the coast. Instead, Kenneth had driven southeast on Ortega Highway, leading his wife deep into the mountains toward Lake Elsinore and Riverside County, in completely the opposite direction from their home.

Friends and colleagues began painting a picture of the Stahls as a successful professional couple who seemed to have everything. Kenneth came from a distinguished medical family, with his father having been a prominent surgeon who set high expectations for his son. After earning his medical degree in 1968, Kenneth had built a respected practice as an anesthesiologist, developing a reputation for precision and skill that led to his appointment to the state medical board.

Carolyn had left her home state of Michigan to establish herself in California, building a thriving optometry practice in Long Beach, where patients praised her gentle manner and meticulous attention to their care. She had developed an especially close relationship with Kenneth's mother, often referring to the extended Stahl family as her "California family" and spending holidays with them when she couldn't travel back to Michigan.

The couple had married on New Year's Day, 1988, in a Las Vegas ceremony that friends described as romantic and spontaneous. They had no children together, though Kenneth maintained minimal contact with an adult son from a previous marriage who lived in Texas. To outsiders, they appeared to be living the California dream in one of Orange County's most exclusive communities, enjoying the rewards of their successful medical careers.

But investigators soon discovered that, beneath this polished surface, the Stahl marriage had been troubled for years.

Carolyn's friends initially spoke in careful, measured tones about the deceased couple, but as investigators pressed for details, troubling information began to emerge. Kenneth had been involved in multiple affairs throughout their marriage; Carolyn had discovered the first one in the mid-1990s, when she'd found credit card receipts for hotels and restaurants she'd never visited. The discovery had devastated her, but she had chosen to stay in the marriage, convinced that Kenneth would change if she just tried hard enough to be the perfect wife.

"She went to marriage counseling, both alone and with Kenneth," one friend explained, "and she really believed they could work through it if she just loved him enough."

Instead of confronting Kenneth directly about his continued infidelities, Carolyn had found other ways to cope: extensive shopping sprees that filled multiple closets in their home. Her collection contained over thirty thousand dollars in clothes and accessories, many with tags still attached, representing years of what she privately called "retail revenge" for her husband's betrayals. When friends asked about the expensive items, she would claim they were gifts from her loving husband, maintaining the image of a happy marriage even to those closest to her.

Kenneth's colleagues painted a different picture of the anesthesiologist, describing a man who had been struggling with serious health problems for decades. He had suffered his first heart attack at thirty-seven, followed by multiple cardiac procedures over the years that had left him increasingly obsessed with his mortality. Just four months before his death, in July 1999, he had undergone quadruple bypass surgery with only a twenty percent chance of survival. Although he had beaten those odds, he had also emerged from the experience convinced that time was running out.

"He talked constantly about feeling trapped," a fellow physician recalled, "like he was running out of time to live the life he really wanted."

The marriage had essentially become a business arrangement by 1999, with Kenneth and Carolyn sharing a house and attending social functions together while living entirely separate emotional lives. They maintained appearances for their professional reputations and social standing, but intimacy and genuine connection had died years earlier.

Three days after the murders, investigators pulled Kenneth's cell phone records and discovered a pattern that immediately caught their attention. One number appeared repeatedly in the weeks leading up to his death: Adriana Vasco. On November 20 alone, Kenneth had called her five times, including calls made shortly before his death. The frequency and timing of these calls suggested something far more significant than casual friendship.

Investigators recognized Adriana Vasco's name from their preliminary interviews. She was a thirty-three-year-old medical secretary who had worked at one of Kenneth's affiliated medical offices years earlier. When contacted for an interview, she agreed immediately, arriving at the sheriff's station nervous but seemingly eager to help.

She explained that she had known Dr. Stahl since 1992, when she worked as his receptionist, and they had remained friends over the years. Kenneth sometimes helped her with computer problems because he was tech-savvy and generous with his expertise. Their relationship was purely professional and friendly, nothing more.

"When did you last speak with him?" the detective asked.

"The morning of November 20," she replied quickly. "He called about a computer issue I was having with my home system."

"Did he mention his plans for that evening?"

"He said he was taking his wife out for her birthday but hadn't decided where yet. He seemed normal, just like always."

The detectives thanked her for her time, and she left, but something about the interview felt wrong. Her answers had come too quickly, as if she had rehearsed them, and her body language suggested someone hiding significant information. The sheer volume of phone calls between her and Kenneth indicated a relationship far more involved than computer troubleshooting would require.

———

Weeks passed without significant progress as the Sheriff's Department invested substantial resources in the investigation. Detectives conducted dozens of interviews with friends, family members, and colleagues, but no clear motive emerged for why someone would want both doctors dead. The excessive violence suggested rage and personal connection, but investigators couldn't identify anyone with sufficient reason to commit such a brutal double murder.

Carolyn's sister, Linda, called the department regularly, desperate for any news about the investigation. Kenneth's family struggled to understand what had happened on that dark mountain road. The case was growing cold, and investigators feared they might never find the killer.

In February 2000, detectives decided to re-interview Adriana Vasco, this time armed with more information about her relationship with Kenneth. Witnesses had reported seeing them together at restaurants and coffee shops, meetings that seemed more intimate than professional. The phone records showed patterns of communication that suggested daily contact, sometimes multiple calls within hours.

Confronted with this evidence, Adriana's story began to shift like sand beneath the investigators' questions.

"Okay, yes, we had an affair," she admitted, her voice barely above a whisper. "But it ended in 1996, when I realized he would never leave his wife."

"Why did you think he would leave her?" the detective pressed.

"He told me he was unhappy, that his marriage was over in everything but name. But then his mother got involved, and she loved Carolyn, and Kenneth couldn't disappoint his mother. So I ended it."

"But you stayed in contact?"

"As friends only. He helped me financially sometimes when things were tight, and he was always there when I needed advice or support. But the romantic part was over."

She left after two hours of questioning, and while investigators had more information about the relationship, they still had no clear connection to the murders. Many people have affairs without resorting to murder, and the relationship had supposedly ended three years before the killings.

―――――

By September 2000, the case had stalled completely, with no new leads and no clear direction for the investigation. In October, the Sheriff's Department decided to have the cold case unit take a fresh look at all the evidence, going back to the beginning with eyes unclouded by the previous months of dead ends.

The detectives assigned to the cold case started with the phone records, examining them from a new perspective. This time, they noticed something the original investigators had overlooked: Kenneth's calls to Adriana followed a specific pattern, intensifying dramatically in early November. They also discovered calls between Adriana and another number registered to someone named Tony Satton. The phone's billing address was the same Anaheim apartment complex where Adriana lived.

A search for Tony Satton revealed no legitimate history anywhere in Orange County. No driver's license existed under that name, no employment records, no credit history, and no previous addresses. The name appeared to be an alias, carefully chosen to avoid detection.

Investigators obtained a warrant to search a storage unit that Adriana had been renting for several months. Inside, among boxes of clothing and old furniture, they discovered items that changed the entire direction of the investigation: a photograph of a man they didn't recognize, another photo showing the same man with Adriana at what appeared to be a casual dinner, and most shocking of all, California DMV driver's license photos of both Kenneth and Carolyn Stahl.

The presence of these official ID photos raised an immediate and chilling question: Why would Adriana have photographs of the murder victims' identification documents hidden in her storage unit?

The man in the photographs was identified through law enforcement databases as Dennis Earl Godley, a thirty-year-old career criminal from North Carolina whose record stretched back to his teenage years. His rap sheet included robbery, assault, weapons charges, and multiple escape attempts that had earned him the nickname "Weasel" among North Carolina law enforcement for his ability to slip away from custody.

In August 1999, just three months before the murders, Dennis had escaped from police custody in Suffolk, Virginia, during a robbery arrest. He had fled across the country to California, settling in Anaheim under the assumed name Tony Satton and finding work as a maintenance man at the apartment complex where Adriana lived. He had kept a low profile, paying cash for everything and avoiding any situation that might require legitimate identification.

Dennis Godley

Residents of the apartment complex remembered him as a quiet man who was good at fixing things and seemed to keep to himself—except for his relationship with Adriana. They had started dating in September 1999 after he repaired her kitchen sink, and neighbors described them as an unexpected couple. She was outgoing and talkative, while he remained reserved and watchful, always seeming to scan his surroundings for potential threats.

Adriana's former supervisor, Susana Torres-Bivian, provided information that fundamentally changed investigators' understanding of the case. In the summer of 1999, Adriana had confided that she was dating two men simultaneously: Dr. Stahl and a man named Tony. More surprisingly, Adriana had claimed that both men not only knew about each other but had accepted the unusual arrangement.

"She said they were both fine with it," Torres-Bivian recalled, "which seemed strange to me, but Adriana insisted it was all very civilized and modern."

If Kenneth knew about Dennis, and Dennis knew about Kenneth, investigators wondered what possible connection could exist between a respected doctor and a fugitive criminal beyond their shared relationship with Adriana.

Investigators began examining Kenneth's financial records with renewed scrutiny, looking for any unusual transactions in the months before his death. On November 1, 1999, they found what they were looking for: Kenneth had withdrawn $20,000 in cash from his checking account, a transaction completely out of character for a man who paid for everything with credit cards and kept meticulous financial records. The executor of his estate had been unable to account for this money, and it had never surfaced in any of Kenneth's known accounts or purchases.

Around the same time as Kenneth's withdrawal, Adriana had suddenly appeared at work wearing expensive jewelry that coworkers couldn't help but notice. When asked about the dramatic change in her accessories, she'd claimed that Tony had bought the pieces for her, explaining that his wealthy parents regularly sent him money from their successful business back east.

Investigators quickly confirmed that Dennis Godley's family lived in a modest trailer in rural North Carolina, surviving on disability payments and food stamps. They had no money to send anyone, let alone enough to purchase thousands of dollars in jewelry.

Jim Stewart came forward with information that added another crucial piece to the puzzle. As the grandfather of Adriana's daughter from a previous relationship, he had maintained regular contact with her over the years. In August 1999, he had accompanied Adriana to a gun store where she was supposedly looking for personal protection. She had pointed to a .357 caliber revolver in the display case and casually mentioned that she had recently purchased a similar weapon for her boyfriend, Tony.

After the murders became public, Stewart had asked Adriana about the gun during a family gathering. She had seemed flustered by the question and claimed that Tony had returned it to the store because "it wasn't what he wanted after all." The explanation had never sat right with Stewart, and now he felt compelled to share this information with investigators.

The evidence was entirely circumstantial but painted a compelling picture: Kenneth's money had disappeared at the same time Adriana had suddenly procured expensive jewelry, she had purchased a gun matching the type used in the murders, and she had photos of the victims' identification hidden in her storage unit. The investigation was finally moving forward.

In August 2000, nine months after the murders, Dennis Godley made a fatal mistake. Believing enough time had passed for the heat to die down, he had returned to North Carolina to stay with family members in rural Pitt County.

Sergeant Ron Smith of the Pitt County Sheriff's Department received a tip about Godley's location from a confidential informant who knew about the outstanding warrants.

Eight deputies and a tracking dog surrounded the trailer where Dennis's father lived on a humid August morning. Dennis tried to escape through a back window, but he was quickly apprehended by deputies who had anticipated this move. He was arrested on the outstanding robbery charges from Virginia, having no idea that California investigators were building a murder case against him.

Meanwhile, Adriana had been arrested in late November 2000 on misdemeanor warrants for DUI and traffic violations that had accumulated over several months. She was being held in Los Angeles County Jail when investigators made a strategic decision to apply pressure through an unexpected source.

A detective phoned Greg Stewart, another of Adriana's boyfriends and the father of her daughter, with carefully chosen information. The detective warned Greg that they had located Tony Satton, whose real name was Dennis Godley, and suggested that some of Godley's criminal associates might pose a danger to anyone connected to him.

Greg, genuinely panicked by this news, immediately called Adriana in jail to warn her.

"They found Tony," he said urgently. "The detective says he's talking to them about everything."

Within hours of that phone call, Adriana called the detective herself, her voice transformed by desperation and fear. She wanted to meet immediately, saying she had information about the Stahl murders that investigators needed to know.

On the evening of November 27, 2000, Adriana Vasco sat across from two detectives in an interview room at the Los Angeles County Jail. For the next several hours, she would unveil a conspiracy that had been months in the planning, though she carefully painted herself as a reluctant participant trapped between two dangerous men who had left her no choice.

According to Adriana, the seeds of murder had been planted years earlier, when Kenneth first began complaining about his marriage. He had talked about divorce but claimed it would destroy him financially, despite the existence of a prenuptial agreement. More importantly, he couldn't bear to disappoint his mother, who had embraced Carolyn as the daughter she'd never had.

Kenneth's first attempt to find someone to kill his wife had occurred in early 1999, when he approached an electrician named Richard Anaya, a former gang member who had turned his life around through faith. Kenneth had offered him $75,000 to kill Carolyn, suggesting various methods, including making it look like a carjacking or a home invasion. Richard had refused and offered to pray with Kenneth instead, a suggestion the doctor had declined.

Undeterred by this rejection, Kenneth had turned to the one person he trusted completely: Adriana. He knew about her connections to people on the margins of society, people who might be willing to do things others wouldn't. Find someone, he had told her repeatedly. Find someone who could solve his problem permanently.

In September 1999, fate had seemed to provide an answer when Dennis Godley fixed Adriana's kitchen sink. They had started dating, and during one night spent drinking and using drugs, Dennis had boasted about his criminal past, claiming membership in a group of professional killers in North Carolina. Adriana, perhaps testing his truthfulness or trying to impress him with her own connections, had mentioned that she knew a doctor who wanted his wife dead.

Dennis's reaction had been immediate and terrifying. His entire demeanor had changed as he insisted on meeting this doctor, seeing an opportunity for a significant payday. When Adriana had hesitated, expressing doubts about getting involved in something so serious, Dennis had grabbed her arm hard enough to leave bruises and threatened to kill her and her children if she didn't arrange the meeting.

"I was trapped," Adriana told the detectives, tears streaming down her face. "Kenneth wouldn't give up the idea no matter how many times I tried to talk him out of it, and Dennis made it clear he would hurt my family if I didn't help him."

Kenneth and Dennis had met in a Huntington Beach parking lot in early November, with Adriana serving as the reluctant intermediary. Kenneth had handed over $30,000 in cash—the $20,000 from his bank withdrawal, plus another $10,000 from a source Adriana claimed not to know. The plan they developed was supposed to be simple: Dennis would ambush the couple on a remote road, killing Carolyn while making it look like a random attack. Kenneth would play the role of the traumatized widower who had barely escaped with his life.

On November 19, the three conspirators had driven out to Ortega Highway to scout the location for the next night's crime. Dennis had chosen a spot near an emergency call box, isolated enough to avoid witnesses but accessible enough that Kenneth could reasonably claim they had stopped for car trouble. Dennis had fired his gun at a road sign, both testing the weapon and marking the exact spot where Kenneth should stop the following night.

Adriana claimed she had made one last attempt to stop the plan, telling Kenneth that Dennis was dangerous and unpredictable—that once violence was unleashed, it couldn't be controlled. Kenneth had remained silent, his jaw set with determination, his commitment to the murderous plan absolute.

The next morning, November 20, Kenneth had called Adriana one final time, and she had heard uncertainty in his voice for the first time since the planning had begun. For a brief moment, she had thought he might cancel everything, might choose divorce over death. But by evening, he had steeled himself for what was to come, taking Carolyn to dinner for her birthday and playing the role of the loving husband one last time.

While the Stahls dined at the Mexican restaurant, Adriana and Dennis waited at a gas station along Ortega Highway. When Dennis spotted the Stahls' car passing their location, he directed Adriana to follow at a distance, keeping their headlights off until the last moment.

Kenneth had pulled over at the predetermined spot exactly as planned, using the emergency call box as his landmark in the darkness.

"I stayed in the car," Adriana told the detectives, her voice barely audible. "I heard the shots, so many shots, and I heard Carolyn screaming. It was horrible, nothing like what was supposed to happen."

Dennis had approached the Stahls' vehicle with the .357 revolver that Adriana had obtained for him weeks earlier. The plan had called for him to shoot Carolyn through the window while Kenneth kept his hands visible on the steering wheel, establishing his innocence.

But something had gone wrong from the very first moment.

Maybe Kenneth had moved his hands involuntarily, maybe Dennis had never intended to leave witnesses regardless of the plan, or maybe jealousy over Adriana had driven him to eliminate his rival. Whatever the reason, Dennis had shot both occupants of the car, firing again and again until his gun was empty.

After the initial volley, he'd had to return to Adriana's car to reload, his movements calm and methodical. She had started to drive away in panic, but Dennis had pointed the gun at her head and spoken with chilling clarity.

She told detectives, "He said he'd pop me if I moved, that he'd kill me right there and leave my body with theirs."

Dennis had returned to the Stahls' car and fired more shots, ensuring both victims were dead beyond any possibility of survival. When he returned to Adriana's car for the final time, he had been almost cheerful, explaining his actions as if they had been entirely reasonable.

"He said Kenneth didn't follow instructions, that he couldn't leave witnesses who might identify him later. He said it was Kenneth's own fault for not doing exactly what he was told."

They had driven back to Anaheim in complete silence. Days later, Adriana had driven Dennis to Huntington Beach Pier in the early morning hours, where he had thrown the murder weapon into the ocean, watching it disappear beneath the dark waves. Within weeks, he had fled California entirely, returning to North Carolina while Adriana maintained her silence and prayed the investigation would never lead to her.

———

On December 12, 2000, the Orange County District Attorney filed formal charges against Adriana Vasco and Dennis Godley: two counts of first-degree murder each, with special circumstances of multiple murder, murder for financial gain, and lying in wait. The special circumstances made both defendants eligible for the death penalty under California law.

The case that had baffled investigators for over a year had finally been solved, revealing a twisted plot where the mastermind had become a victim of his own conspiracy. Kenneth Stahl, the respected doctor who had hired someone to kill his wife, had died believing he could control violence like he controlled anesthesia levels in an operating room, discovering too late that murder follows no one's rules.

Two days before Christmas, Orange County Register reporter Bill Rams visited Adriana in jail for an exclusive interview. Unaware that her confession to police would later be ruled inadmissible due to Miranda violations, she spoke freely about the events on Ortega Highway, providing details that would become crucial evidence at her trial.

———

Adriana Vasco's trial began in November 2002, with prosecutors presenting a mountain of circumstantial evidence: phone records showing hundreds of calls between the conspirators, financial documents tracking Kenneth's money to Adriana's jewelry, witness testimony about the relationships between all three participants, and most damning of all, her own words to reporter Bill Rams describing her presence at the murder scene.

Her defense team argued she suffered from battered woman syndrome, psychologically unable to resist the demands of violent men due to a lifetime of abuse. They painted her as a victim herself, caught between Kenneth's obsession and Dennis's threats, unable to save anyone—including herself.

The jury deliberated for days before returning their verdict on November 26, 2002: guilty of first-degree murder for Carolyn's death and second-degree murder for Kenneth's death. The distinction in the verdicts suggested that although they believed Adriana had actively planned Carolyn's killing, Kenneth's death, while foreseeable, hadn't been part of the original scheme.

"She was a pretty tough, street-smart person," juror Donald Tobias explained to reporters afterward. "We felt that as long as she wasn't intoxicated or high, she had a pretty good idea this would happen."

On January 24, 2003, Judge Francisco Briseno sentenced Adriana to life in prison without the possibility of parole. She wept as the sentence was read, her sister Norma sobbing in the gallery as she realized Adriana would never come home to her children.

Dennis Godley avoided trial by pleading guilty in May 2004, accepting life without parole in exchange for prosecutors removing the death penalty from consideration. During his plea, his attorney made a shocking last-minute claim: Dennis had only killed Kenneth, and it was actually Adriana who had shot Carolyn. No evidence supported this assertion, and prosecutors dismissed it as a desperate attempt to muddy waters that were already clear.

Dennis died in prison years later from cancer, taking any remaining secrets about that night to his grave. Adriana remains incarcerated at the Central California Women's Facility in Chowchilla, where she will spend the rest of her life contemplating how a birthday surprise became a death trap on a dark mountain road, and how a plan for one murder became two.

CHAPTER 8
THE PLASTIC ROSES

The temperature had already climbed past ninety degrees when Investigator Gregory Frenzel arrived at 301 Pickett Court in Berryville, Virginia, on Thursday, July 30, 2009. He was responding to a welfare check requested by Gail Smith's aunt in New Jersey, who hadn't heard from her niece since Sunday evening—four days of silence from a woman who typically returned calls within hours.

Berryville was a quiet town of about three thousand people in Clarke County, the kind of place where major crime was rare and neighbors knew each other by name. Frenzel had been with the department for twenty years, and most welfare checks ended with relief—someone had taken an unexpected trip or forgotten to charge their phone.

The house was a brick ranch built in the 1960s, typical of the neighborhood. What wasn't typical was the state of the garden. Gail Smith was known throughout the neighborhood for her meticulous gardens, but now tomatoes hung overripe on their vines, zucchini had grown grotesquely large, and the prized sunflowers had begun to droop. Mail overflowed from the box at the street.

Frenzel knocked on the front door. No answer. He knocked again, harder, identifying himself as Berryville Police. The neighborhood was silent except for the constant hum of air conditioners battling the July heat. Through the decorative glass panels flanking the door, he could see into the entranceway. The shape on the floor was unmistakably human and unmistakably still.

He radioed for backup and checked the perimeter of the house. The back door was locked with no signs of forced entry. Windows were intact and secured from the inside. Returning to the front, Frenzel made the decision to force entry. The door frame splintered.

The smell of decomposition hit immediately, intensified by the extreme heat. The house interior was well over one hundred degrees. Someone had turned off the air conditioning in the middle of a Virginia summer. Gail Smith lay on her back about ten feet from the door, her body showing advanced decomposition from what appeared to be several days in the heat. Dark staining surrounded the body where fluids had leaked into the hardwood floor.

A single gunshot wound marked her left temple. The stippling around the wound indicated a contact shot—the gun had been pressed directly against her head. No defensive wounds were visible on her hands or arms. Beside the body, placed with apparent care, sat a bouquet of plastic roses. Bright red, obviously artificial, and completely out of place.

Frenzel secured the scene and waited for backup. Within thirty minutes, the quiet residential street had transformed into a major crime scene. Yellow tape created a perimeter.

The medical examiner arrived, followed by crime scene technicians and additional detectives. Neighbors gathered beyond the tape, some crying, others standing in shocked silence.

Gail Smith had lived in Berryville for sixteen years, moving there in 1993 after retiring from a thirty-year career as a flight attendant with TWA. At fifty-nine, she'd traded constant travel for deep roots in a small community. She'd bought the house on Pickett Court and immediately began transforming the yard into elaborate gardens that became a neighborhood attraction.

She hadn't been content with quiet retirement. Within a year of arriving, she was volunteering at the Barns of Rose Hill, a cultural center in a restored barn. She helped establish an Alzheimer's care program at Grace Episcopal Church, drawing on personal experience as her father's mind deteriorated from the disease. In 2008, she successfully ran for town council, winning by a significant margin.

The medical examiner determined that death had occurred on July 26, a Sunday morning. The weapon was a .22-caliber handgun. The bullet had not exited, remaining lodged in the skull. No shell casing was found at the scene, suggesting the killer had either used a revolver or collected the evidence.

The deliberately disabled air conditioning appeared to be an attempt to accelerate decomposition and destroy forensic evidence. It showed planning and forethought, not a crime of passion.

Friends told investigators that Gail despised artificial flowers. She grew real roses in her backyard and gave away bouquets throughout the summer. The plastic roses at the crime scene were completely inconsistent with everything they knew about her.

The investigation into Gail's background revealed a complex family situation centered around money and old resentments. Her father, Timothy Smith Sr., was in his eighties and deep in the grip of Alzheimer's disease. He lived in a care facility in Winchester, about fifteen miles from Berryville, where Gail visited him daily, even though he no longer recognized her.

Timothy Sr. had been a successful businessman, accumulating assets worth approximately $750,000 through real estate investments and careful saving. It was a fortune by any standard, but especially significant in rural Virginia.

Gail held power of attorney over her father's affairs. She managed his medical care, paid for the nursing facility, handled his investments, and made all financial decisions. According to the will, drafted when Timothy Sr. still had his mental faculties, Gail would inherit virtually everything when he died. The house, the investments, the remaining properties—all would go to her.

Her siblings, Timothy Jr. and Deborah, would each receive exactly one dollar.

Not nothing, which might have been contested as an oversight. One dollar each—deliberate, specific, and humiliating. The will even included language explaining that the token amount was intentional; both children had been considered and found wanting.

Two weeks before her death, Gail had told a neighbor something troubling. If anything happened to her, she said, the police should look at her brother Tim. The neighbor had thought it was just family drama related to the inheritance dispute. After the murder, this warning took on new significance, and the neighbor immediately reported it to the police.

———

Timothy Smith Jr. lived in Burkeville, Virginia, 127 miles south of Berryville. The drive would take over two hours on rural roads. At fifty-six, he was partially paralyzed on his left side and had developed a reputation as a heavy drinker with a violent temper.

When detectives arrived on August 1, Tim had his alibi prepared. He'd been home all day on July 26. Phone records showed he'd made several calls from his landline that morning. A neighbor had seen him on his porch that afternoon, though she couldn't specify exact times. His mobility issues would make a 250-mile round trip difficult and noticeable.

Tim didn't hide his anger about the will, calling it theft and manipulation, but he denied any involvement in Gail's death.

Deborah Smith, sixty-two, lived in an apartment complex in Farmville, about forty miles from Tim. She worked as a receptionist at a medical office. When investigators interviewed her on August 2, she presented herself as shocked but not entirely surprised.

Deborah's alibi for July 26 was solid. She'd attended the 9:00 a.m. service at her church, where dozens of people saw her.

After church, she'd gone to lunch with three friends. The receipt showed they'd paid at 1:47 p.m. She'd then gone home, where a neighbor saw her carrying groceries inside at around 3:00 p.m.

Both siblings expressed anger about the will, though in different ways. Tim was openly bitter. Deborah was more subtle, suggesting their father hadn't been competent when he'd changed the will to favor Gail, hinting at undue influence without making direct accusations.

By September 2009, the investigation had hit a wall. The crime scene, compromised by heat and decomposition, had yielded limited forensic evidence. The .22-caliber bullet recovered from Gail's skull was too damaged for ballistic comparison without a weapon to match it against. The plastic roses had been purchased from a dollar store, but there were dozens of locations throughout Virginia, and they were a common item sold for cash with no way to trace the buyer.

Frenzel had a victim, a motive, and two suspects with solid alibis. He'd interviewed everyone in Gail's orbit. All told the same story: Gail was kind, dedicated, and well-liked. No enemies except possibly her own family.

The detective kept Gail's photograph on his desk with a simple note: "Who killed this beautiful woman?"

October came and went. Officially, the case was still active, but it was going cold.

The break came in November 2009. Tim Smith Jr. was in jail, serving ninety days for assault—a bar fight that violated his probation from an earlier drunk and disorderly conviction. His cellmate at Farmville Correctional Center contacted authorities through his lawyer with information about Tim talking about a plot to kill his sister using snake venom.

This led investigators to a man named Edward Poley. When detectives found him living in a trailer park twenty miles from Tim's house, Poley seemed to have been expecting them.

Poley explained that he'd rented a room from Tim after going through a divorce in 2008. For the first few months, things were fine. Tim drank too much and complained about his family, but he was a decent enough landlord. Then, in May of that same year, Tim had laid out a detailed plan to kill Gail using rattlesnake venom.

According to Poley, Tim had researched everything: where to buy rattlesnakes, how to milk them for venom, and how much would be fatal. The plan was to inject the venom between Gail's toes, where nobody would see the puncture mark. It would look like cardiac arrest, Tim had explained, because snake venom breaks down quickly in a dead body.

Tim had offered Poley $2,000 plus six months of free rent to help execute the plan. Poley had packed his belongings and left within a week, too frightened to stay. He hadn't reported it, fearing both Tim's temper and being implicated himself.

Armed with Poley's testimony, prosecutors charged Tim Smith Jr. with solicitation to commit murder for the 2008 plot. On December 15, 2009, faced with the testimony and possibility of a longer sentence at trial, Tim pleaded guilty. He received two years in state prison.

The plea agreement included an admission that he had solicited Edward Poley to assist in murdering Gail Smith by means of injecting her with rattlesnake venom. It proved Tim had been planning to kill his sister for at least a year before her actual death.

However, Frenzel knew this was just the beginning. The snake plot had failed, but someone had succeeded in killing Gail on July 26, 2009—and Tim had been home in Burkeville that day, his alibi confirmed by phone records and witnesses.

Two years passed. Tim served his time for solicitation and was released in December 2011. The murder case had officially gone cold, but Frenzel couldn't let it go.

In February 2012, he attended a law enforcement conference where new techniques in cell phone data analysis were demonstrated. Technology had advanced significantly in the few years since 2009, and cell tower data could now be analyzed with much greater precision.

Frenzel obtained fresh warrants for phone records and hired a telecommunications expert. For three days, the expert analyzed data from July 26, 2009. What emerged changed everything.

Tim Smith's landline had made twelve calls to a prepaid cell phone between 8:00 a.m. and noon on July 26. While Tim's phone stayed in Burkeville, the prepaid phone had traveled. Cell tower data showed it moving from Farmville north toward Berryville. At 10:47 a.m., it pinged a tower less than a mile from Gail's house. At 11:15, it began moving south again. By 2:00 p.m., it was back in Farmville.

The pattern was clear: Tim had stayed home to maintain his alibi while directing someone else to commit the murder via phone.

The prepaid phone had been purchased with cash six months before the murder and went completely dark after July 26—except for one mistake. On July 28, two days after the murder, it had made a single call to a local pizzeria in Farmville.

The pizza shop still had records from July 2009, three years earlier. The delivery on July 28 went to an apartment complex on the south side of Farmville. The name on the order was Tony Sharpe.

Tony Sharpe was twenty-six years old in 2009. He had done odd jobs for Tim Smith over the years, but he was struggling financially, with a baby on the way. When investigators found him in September 2012, he was working at a body shop and still living in the same apartment complex.

Tony denied any involvement in the murder, claiming he'd lost the prepaid phone somewhere. Without more evidence, investigators had to let him go, but they kept the pressure on.

The pressure didn't break Tony. It broke Rebecca Morrison, who had been Tony's girlfriend in 2009. She'd left him in 2010 and moved to Richmond. On March 21, 2013, nearly four years after Gail's murder, she walked into the Berryville Police Department.

Rebecca told investigators that on July 26, 2009, Tony came home shaking and drenched in sweat. That afternoon, he'd confessed to her what he had done.

According to Rebecca, Tim had first approached Tony in May 2009 about a job that would solve his money problems. Initial promises of fifty thousand dollars had shrunk to three thousand by July. For someone facing eviction with a baby on the way, three thousand was still significant money.

Tim had given Tony the prepaid phone with instructions to drive to Berryville on July 26. Those twelve calls were Tim directing Tony—where to park, which house, and when to approach. Tony was told to carry plastic flowers as a prop. The flowers and the .22-caliber gun had been provided by Deborah Smith, Tim's sister, who had purchased them specifically for the murder.

Rebecca said Tony had knocked on Gail's door while holding the plastic roses. When Gail had opened the door, he'd forced his way in. When she'd begun to scream, he'd pressed the gun to her temple.

The sound that had followed had haunted him afterward, contributing to the heavy drinking that had eventually ended their relationship.

———

Following Rebecca's confession, Kevin Brinson, a Smith family friend, came forward with information about Deborah Smith. At a family gathering in 2012, after drinking wine, Deborah had made a startling statement: "I bought the bullets and the flowers." She'd said it like she was proud of her role in the murder.

The arrests came quickly. Tony Sharpe was arrested on March 22, 2013, at the body shop where he worked. Tim Smith Jr. was arrested the next day, on March 23, at his home in Burkeville. Deborah Smith was arrested on August 15, 2013, at her apartment.

Faced with strong evidence and the possibility of capital murder charges, all three defendants eventually chose to plead guilty.

Tony Sharpe entered his plea on August 12, 2013, before Judge John E. Wetsel Jr. in Clarke County Circuit Court. He pleaded guilty to first-degree murder, conspiracy to commit murder, and shooting in the commission of a felony. He apologized for taking an innocent life.

Deborah Smith pleaded guilty on April 16, 2014, to felony perjury and misdemeanor obstruction of justice. The perjury charge stemmed from her grand jury testimony denying knowledge of the murder plot. While prosecutors believed she'd been central to planning the murder, they accepted the plea deal based on what they could prove.

Tim Smith Jr. pleaded guilty on February 12, 2015, to first-degree murder, conspiracy to commit first-degree murder, and use of a firearm in the commission of a felony. His attorney attempted to shift blame to his co-conspirators, but the strategy didn't affect the outcome.

Judge Wetsel imposed significant sentences. Tim Smith Jr., sixty-two at sentencing in March 2015, received twenty-three years—twenty for murder and conspiracy running concurrently, plus three consecutive years for the firearm charge. His earliest release date would be April 12, 2033, when he will be eighty.

Tony Sharpe, twenty-nine at sentencing in April 2015, received twenty-five years. His release date of September 2036 means he'll be in his fifties when freed.

Deborah Smith received eight years—seven for perjury, one for obstruction. She has since been released, the only conspirator to regain freedom. Many observers felt the sentence was too lenient for someone they believed had orchestrated the conspiracy.

———

Timothy Smith Sr., unaware that his daughter had been murdered, died on February 23, 2010, while Tim Jr. was serving time for solicitation. The $750,000 estate didn't go to Tim or Deborah. Since Gail had predeceased her father without children, the inheritance went to Timothy Sr.'s sister in South Carolina.

Tim Jr. and Deborah received exactly what the will specified: one dollar each.

They had conspired to murder their sister for an inheritance they were never going to receive. Even if they hadn't been caught, the money would have gone to their aunt. The murder was not just evil but pointless.

Detective Gregory Frenzel removed Gail's photograph from his desk after the final sentencing in 2015. The case that had consumed six years was finally closed. Three people had conspired to kill a woman over money, destroying multiple lives in the process.

In Berryville, Gail Smith is remembered for her community service and her gardens. The Alzheimer's program she helped establish at Grace Episcopal Church continues to operate, and the town council established a memorial scholarship in her name for students interested in public service.

CHAPTER 9
THE BARGAIN BASEMENT

The basement was wrong for surgery. Everything about it was wrong.

Paramedics from the West Seneca Volunteer Fire Department, New York, would later struggle to describe what they found when they burst through the door on August 25, 1997. A young woman lay dying on a makeshift operating table, her skin taking on the blue-gray pallor that meant oxygen starvation. Blood pooled beneath inadequate surgical draping. The smell of panic and medical disinfectant hung thick in the air.

However, what made first responders stop in their tracks wasn't the dying patient or the cramped, makeshift surgical suite. It was what the doctor was holding: a wire coat hanger, bent and twisted, that he was attempting to force down the woman's throat in a desperate bid to create an airway.

Sarah Smith had walked into this West Seneca office eight hours earlier for what she believed would be a routine breast augmentation. For months, she had set aside what little she could, persuaded by ads for cut-rate cosmetic surgery. At twenty-six, with a young child, the promise of transformation was irresistible. The doctor seemed larger than life—cruising the streets of Buffalo in a red Lamborghini, smiling from television screens as he praised his so-called revolutionary hair system. His name was Dr. Anthony Pignataro, and he would later tell investigators that everything had been under control.

Everything had not been under control.

———

The story begins decades earlier, in the shadow of a different kind of success. Anthony's father, Ralph Pignataro, was everything a Buffalo doctor should be: respected, competent, and trusted by generations of families. Anthony watched and wanted.

At the prestigious Nichols School, Anthony told everyone he would be a doctor. Not just any doctor, but a surgeon. The rejections started arriving in his senior year at Lehigh University. Cornell: rejected. Columbia: rejected. University at Buffalo, where his father's name carried weight: rejected. His MCAT scores were mediocre. His grades were uninspiring.

But Anthony had met Deborah Rago at Lehigh in 1978, and she believed in him. She was working as a pharmacy technician, practical and grounded where Anthony was grandiose and dreaming. They'd fallen in love dancing to Donna Summer's "Last Dance" at a college party.

"Puerto Rico," he told her one evening in 1981. "There's a medical school there. San Juan Bautista. They'll take me."

San Juan Bautista School of Medicine was not accredited by mainland accreditation bodies. It existed for students like Anthony: those with the ambition but not the academic credentials for traditional programs. The instruction was in Spanish, which Anthony barely spoke. But at the end, if you passed, you got an MD degree.

Anthony Pignataro

Deborah married him in 1985, when she was twenty-one and he was finally Dr. Anthony Pignataro. Within a year, she found him with another woman. Her father told her to forgive once. She was pregnant with their first child, and she forgave.

The residency years traced a pattern of failure. At Mercy Ambulatory Care Center from 1987 to 1988, Anthony worked emergency room shifts. An elderly man came in with classic symptoms of bacterial endocarditis. Anthony diagnosed him with the flu and sent him home. The man died three days later. The hospital quietly settled for $100,000.

Georgetown University Hospital accepted Anthony for an otolaryngology residency in 1988. He lasted less than two years. Faculty complaints piled up: chronically late, unprepared, unable to answer basic questions. He transferred to Thomas Jefferson University Hospital in Philadelphia in 1990. On a five-point scale where four was required to continue, Anthony scored 2.4. On national exams, he scored in the twentieth percentile.

In 1991, facing the end of his medical career before it began, Anthony forged an American Board of Otolaryngology diploma. With this document, he obtained temporary privileges at a small hospital. It was the first of many deceptions.

Back in Buffalo by 1992, four different hospitals rejected his applications for privileges. However, Anthony had a solution: If hospitals wouldn't have him, he'd create his own.

The office at 3085 Seneca Street in West Seneca had been a dentist's office. The basement could be converted into something resembling an operating room. He installed basic equipment, but no ventilator, no advanced monitoring equipment, no crash cart. For staff, he hired a licensed practical nurse, not the registered nurses required for surgery. His wife Deborah assisted, though she had no formal medical training. Later, he'd add a seventeen-year-old high school student as an intern.

But Anthony had confidence that overcame these deficiencies. He advertised aggressively. Breast augmentation for half what hospital surgeons charged. Tummy tucks at bargain prices. He bought that red Lamborghini and made sure to park it prominently. He wore expensive suits and a gold Rolex.

His most famous creation was the Snap-On Hair System. The procedure involved surgically implanting titanium posts directly into the skull. Once healed, these posts would hold gold snaps for a hairpiece. Anthony had been his own first patient, having lost his hair at twenty-three. Late-night infomercials showed him demonstrating the system. He became, in Buffalo terms, a minor celebrity.

Terri LaMarti had been saving for two years. The thirty-nine-year-old UPS administrative technician and mother of four decided to treat herself to a tummy tuck at Dr. Pignataro's bargain prices.

What happened during her August 1997 procedure would later be described by investigators as a cascade of medical errors. The incision was too deep. When Anthony encountered bleeding, he simply pulled the tissue tighter, suturing with such force that the blood supply was compromised. His scalpel nicked her intestine, creating a perforation that would lead to infection.

When Terri woke, blood was seeping through the dressings, pooling on the floor. Her surgical incision was gaping open —four inches across, half an inch deep. Anthony dismissed the family's concerns with irritation and demanded they take her home.

At home, blood pooled at Terri's feet. At Mercy Hospital, emergency room nurses gasped when they removed the dressings. One nurse began crying. Another said the wound looked like Terri had been "attacked by a bear."

At 2:30 that morning, Anthony appeared in her hospital room. He had no privileges at Mercy Hospital. He grabbed her chart and began shouting at her to leave before security removed him from the building.

In follow-up visits held at his office, his treatment grew bizarre. When removing her surgical staples, he reached into his desk drawer and pulled out an office staple remover—the kind used for paper. He proceeded to extract the medical staples with this office supply while Terri watched in horror.

She would require thirteen corrective surgeries, but Terri LaMarti survived.

———

August 25, 1997, started like any Monday for Sarah Smith. She kissed her two young children goodbye. Her husband had taken the day off to watch them. The surgery was scheduled for 9:00 a.m.

The West Seneca office was quiet when Sarah arrived. Anthony greeted her himself, walking her through the transumbilical breast augmentation procedure one more time. In the basement surgical suite, Deborah Pignataro struggled with the IV line as the teenage intern arranged instruments. There was no anesthesiologist—Anthony handled anesthesia himself to save money.

The initial sedation went smoothly. Anthony administered sodium pentothal and Versed, vital components of surgical anesthesia that work together to induce unconsciousness, relieve anxiety, and block memory of the procedure. He watched as Sarah's eyes closed, then made the incision and began creating the pocket for the implants.

Forty minutes in, Sarah stirred, showing signs of pain despite sedation. A trained anesthesiologist would have recognized this as a critical warning. Instead of stopping to assess her condition, Anthony drew up massive doses of both drugs and pushed them through the IV in quick succession.

Sarah's breathing slowed. Then stopped.

Deborah noticed the color draining from Sarah's lips, replaced by dusky blue. The rise and fall of her chest had stopped, but the basement had no proper monitoring equipment, so no alarms had sounded.

Anthony grabbed an Ambu bag but couldn't get a seal on Sarah's airway. Her tongue had fallen back, blocking the passage. He needed to intubate her, but he had no laryngoscope and no proper tubes.

In desperation, Anthony ran to a closet and grabbed a wire coat hanger. He began frantically bending it into a shape that could hold open her airway, attempting to force the wire down her throat.

Finally, someone called 911.

The paramedics found Sarah with no pulse, the coat hanger still protruding from her mouth. They immediately took over, managing to restart her heart through CPR and proper intubation, but she had been without oxygen for too long. At the hospital, Sarah slipped into a coma. Three days later, life support was withdrawn. She died surrounded by family, her children too young to understand why Mommy wasn't coming home.

The paramedics were so disturbed that they immediately notified the police. Something was very wrong at 3085 Seneca Street.

West Seneca Police arrived to find Anthony cleaning the surgical suite, mopping blood, disposing of waste, and behaving as if nothing unusual had occurred. When asked what had happened, his response was remarkably casual: Complications happen in surgery.

But this wasn't a hospital. This was a basement.

The investigation peeled back years of deception. Anthony's board certification was fraudulent. His hospital privileges had been revoked everywhere. The medical degree from Puerto Rico was real, but his entire subsequent career was built on lies.

The New York State Health Department suspended Anthony Pignataro's license on September 2, 1997. Their review would document thirty counts of professional misconduct. Then, Terri LaMarti came forward. More women followed. Sophie Butryn, seventy-eight, had nearly died from a botched tummy tuck. In total, investigators identified fourteen women who had suffered serious complications.

The medical examiner's report was damning: Sarah had died of asphyxiation due to improper ventilation during anesthesia. The levels of sodium pentothal and Versed were noted as "grossly excessive."

Erie County District Attorney Frank Clark convened a grand jury—the first time in Western New York a physician would be prosecuted for homicide in a patient's death. While waiting to testify, Anthony approached Terri LaMarti in the courthouse hallway, smiling broadly. He tried to hug her and said, "Oh my God, Terri, look at you, you look amazing, I did such a good job."

In August 1998, Anthony pleaded guilty to criminally negligent homicide. Judge Ronald Tills sentenced him to just six months in jail, five years' probation, and permanent loss of his medical license.

"You will never practice medicine again," Judge Tills told him.

With credit for time served, Anthony walked out of jail in December 1998, after serving only four months.

Deborah had stood by Anthony through everything. However, when he came home from jail and she caught him with another woman in January 1999, she kicked him out—only for him to work his way back by June, promising to change.

Deborah's sickness started subtly in May, with what seemed like the flu. Anthony was attentive, cooking elaborate soups he insisted would help her recover. He'd stand over her while she ate, making sure she finished every drop.

But the soup had an odd metallic taste. Their daughter tried a spoonful once and immediately became violently ill. By June, Deborah's hands and feet tingled constantly. Walking became difficult. The symptoms would improve, then worsen dramatically after meals.

Anthony drove her to the hospital in late July. He was unusually insistent and told doctors that Deborah needed her gallbladder removed immediately. The doctors were puzzled—her symptoms didn't match gallbladder disease.

On August 10, 1999, Deborah collapsed at home, legs unable to support her, arms hanging limp. At Mercy Hospital's intensive care unit, Dr. Ronald Moscati ordered a comprehensive toxicology screen.

The results from Albany stunned technicians. Deborah had 29,580 micrograms of arsenic in her system—the highest level the New York State Department of Health had ever recorded. Poison control experts reviewing the data were amazed she was still alive.

Hair follicle analysis revealed systematic poisoning going back to May. The levels increased gradually through June, spiked in July, and reached near-fatal levels in August. The pattern matched perfectly with Anthony's return home and meal preparation.

Police searched the Pignataro home on September 1, 1999. In the garage, they found Terro Ant Killer containing arsenic. Credit card records showed Anthony had purchased it in May, just before Deborah's symptoms began.

When questioned, Anthony didn't deny poisoning his wife. Instead, he said, "Well, I can see how someone could think that."

Their children also tested positive for elevated arsenic levels but recovered after four days of hospitalization. Then, a former cellmate came forward with explosive information. The cellmate told police that while incarcerated in 1998, Anthony Pignataro had asked about poisons, mentioning a girlfriend and a substantial life insurance policy on his wife, Deborah.

Prosecutor Frank Sedita developed a chilling theory. By gradually poisoning Deborah and then convincing doctors to perform surgery, Anthony believed her death would appear to be a surgical complication. Arsenic isn't routinely tested in autopsies.

On May 9, 2000, Anthony Pignataro was arrested for attempted murder. While awaiting trial, investigators discovered he was attempting to arrange a murder-for-hire from jail, targeting the informant.

In November 2000, Anthony pleaded guilty to first-degree assault. Judge Mario Rossetti asked directly: "Did you attempt to cause serious physical injury to your wife by putting arsenic in her food?"

Anthony paused, looked down, and answered softly: "Yes, Your Honor."

The sentence was fifteen years, the maximum. Judge Rossetti declared: "Your life has been a charade of misrepresentation, self-centered, manipulative, with disrespect for the value of human life."

Deborah, now wheelchair-bound from nerve damage, filed for divorce immediately.

Anthony Pignataro served thirteen years of his fifteen-year sentence, maintaining his innocence while claiming Deborah had poisoned herself. When he was released in December 2013, he began planning immediately.

In December 2014, he registered Tony Haute Cosmetique LLC in West Seneca. Two years later, a Florida court approved his legal name change to Anthony T. Haute. He returned to 3085 Seneca Street—where Sarah Smith had died—and launched a website calling himself "Doctor" and "M.D." repeatedly.

His new product was "Plasma Protocol," involving drawing blood and creating personalized cosmetics. The website explained it could only be administered "in the privacy of your own home," adding cryptically, "Unfortunately, I cannot reveal more."

In 2017, WKBW investigative reporter Charlie Specht received a tip: "Anthony Pignataro is practicing medicine again. He calls himself Tony Haute now."

When confronted with cameras, Anthony fled. Within hours, his website vanished.

Erie County DA John Flynn announced, "This man is extremely dangerous. He is a criminal, and the public needs to know about him."

Anthony had already fled to Florida, where he understood the law better than investigators realized. In Florida, someone with a medical degree could call themselves "doctor" without a license—if they included a disclaimer.

In May 2018, marketing professional Sid Klein met "Dr. Tony Haute" about a skincare line. Suspicious, Klein searched the name online and immediately contacted authorities.

The most disturbing discovery: Anthony had created an ElderCare.com profile, advertising as a "trustworthy senior caregiver" with experience "administering medication." No background check required. No disclosure of criminal history.

―――

Today, Anthony Pignataro remains free, now in his seventies, constantly probing for ways to practice his deadly trade. Deborah survives with permanent nerve damage, waking each day with numbness in her limbs. Sarah Smith's children grew up motherless. Terri LaMarti bears thirteen surgical scars.

The basement at 3085 Seneca Street stands empty, but for those who know its history, it represents something darker: where ambition without ability and evil without conscience converged with deadly results.

Prosecutor Frank Sedita once described him simply as "The most narcissistic human being I have ever encountered, and a sociopath."

District Attorney John Flynn's warning still stands: "With nobody keeping an eye on him, I guarantee you he'll hurt somebody else."

The pattern is clear. Anthony Pignataro will practice medicine, or something close enough, until someone stops him. He will use the trust inherent in the title "doctor" as a weapon.

Trying to shove a coat hanger down Sarah Smith's throat went beyond malpractice. It showed just how far Anthony Pignataro would go to defend his fantasy, even if it meant inflicting unbearable suffering.

CHAPTER 10
IMPRINT OF EVIL

The sleeping bag lay in the ditch beside Highway 97 north of Klamath Falls, looking like discarded camping gear to passing motorists. Bruce McDonald slowed his truck, squinting at the bundle through his windshield. His wife, Dorothy, sat beside him, watching as he pulled over.

"Someone must have lost their camping equipment," Dorothy said as Bruce got out to investigate.

It was June 17, 1986, a Tuesday afternoon that would mark the beginning of one of Oregon's most brutal murder investigations. Bruce picked up the sleeping bag and noticed a pillowcase bundled with it. They seemed salvageable, perhaps worth keeping. He put both items in the bed of his truck and drove home with Dorothy.

It wasn't until they examined the items at home that the true horror revealed itself. The sleeping bag was soaked with blood, feces, and semen—not motor oil or camping stains as they'd initially thought. Inside the pillowcase were a woman's purse, identification cards, a checkbook, an address book, a bottle of medication, and a pair of new white sneakers. The identification belonged to someone named Carrie Lynette Love.

Bruce reached for the phone to call the police. This wasn't lost camping gear; this was evidence of something terrible.

Oregon State Police investigators examined the items Bruce McDonald had discovered, spreading them across a table at the Klamath Falls station. The identification in the purse belonged to Carrie Lynette Love, twenty years old, from the Seattle area. The address listed was in Easton, Washington.

An officer picked up the phone and began making calls. The first number he tried from the address book connected him to Kelley Eberle, who identified herself as Carrie's roommate in Seattle.

"Carrie left yesterday morning with her boss, Jesse Pratt," Kelley told him, her voice growing concerned. "He said something about opening a new office in Los Angeles for his trucking company, but Carrie was mainly going to visit her father while they were down there. Is something wrong?"

The officer kept his voice neutral. "We're just trying to locate her. Do you have contact information for her family?"

The next call was to Carrie's father in Los Angeles. The man's voice was already tight with worry when he answered. "I've been trying to reach her since yesterday. She was supposed to call when they got close to L.A. She wanted to visit while she was down here for the business trip."

By evening, investigators had pieced together a basic timeline. Carrie Love had left Seattle on June 16 with her employer, Jesse Pratt, who owned a small trucking company called North Star Trucking. They were supposedly opening a new office in Los Angeles. She'd been expected to call her father, but she never did.

Jesse Pratt

Carrie's boyfriend—a meteorologist she'd met through the National Guard—was the most disturbed by the news. "She didn't want to go," he told the officer. "She was worried about Pratt. She thought he might try something inappropriate. She promised me she'd get out of the truck and call for help if he did anything."

The officer hung up the phone and stared at the bloodstained sleeping bag in the evidence room. A young woman was missing, her belongings abandoned on a remote stretch of highway. Her employer was the last person known to have seen her. And according to everyone the officer had spoken to, Carrie had been afraid of the man she'd gotten into a truck with.

———

Detective Kenneth Cooper had been with the Oregon State Police for twenty-five years. He'd worked over a hundred murder cases, but something about the abandoned belongings on Highway 97 made his jaw clench. The blood on the sleeping bag. The careful placement of the items in the pillowcase, almost as if someone had packed them neatly before discarding them. The location itself—remote, isolated, far from any town.

On the morning of June 18, Cooper returned to the stretch of highway where the McDonalds had made their discovery. He brought Bruce McDonald with him to pinpoint the exact location. The area was part of the Fremont National Forest, thick with pine trees that pressed close to the road. The nearest town was miles away.

"There was a vehicle here yesterday," Bruce mentioned as they stood by the roadside. "A blue International Scout with California plates. It was parked not far from where I found the sleeping bag."

Cooper made a note, though the Scout was long gone now. He organized a search team to comb the area. If Carrie Love's belongings were here, perhaps she was, too.

The search extended south along Highway 97. Cooper drove slowly, checking every turnout, every place where a vehicle might pull off the road. About twenty-five miles south of where the purse had been found, he came upon a truck turnout that was under construction. A massive pile of gravel sat near the edge of the clearing, waiting to be spread.

Cooper got out of his car and walked toward the gravel pile. The area was completely isolated—no buildings, no traffic. Just the forest pressing in on all sides. He circled the pile slowly, his experienced eyes scanning for anything out of place.

That's when he saw it. Protruding from the edge of the gravel pile was a human hand.

Cooper called for backup and began carefully removing the gravel. Within minutes, he'd uncovered the body of a young woman. She was completely nude, her body bearing the signs of horrific violence. Even without seeing the identification photos yet, Cooper knew this was Carrie Love.

The medical examiner would later detail the full extent of the brutality. Carrie had been stabbed multiple times. Deep puncture wounds penetrated her chest. Paper towels and duct tape had been fashioned into a crude mask over her nose and mouth—she'd been asphyxiated. But perhaps most disturbing were the tire marks across her arms and head, indicating she'd been run over by a vehicle after death.

Cooper stood at the scene, taking in every detail. The remote location. The attempt to hide the body under gravel. The separation of the body from the belongings by twenty-five miles. This wasn't a crime of passion or a sudden explosion of violence; someone had methodically tried to cover their tracks.

―――

While Cooper processed the scene, other officers had arrived at the Seattle offices of North Star Trucking. The small company operated out of a run-down building near the waterfront, consisting mainly of one bright green 1976 Kenworth semi-truck and its owner, Jesse Pratt.

The officers were examining the office when the phone rang. One of them answered, and coincidentally, it was Pratt calling to check his messages.

"This is Jesse Pratt," the voice on the other end said. "I'm calling to check in with the office."

The officer identified himself and delivered the news carefully. "Mr. Pratt, we need to speak with you about Carrie Love. She's been found deceased in Oregon."

There was a pause on the line. When Pratt spoke again, his voice sounded strained but controlled. "What? What happened to her?"

"Where are you right now, Mr. Pratt?"

"I'm on my way to Phoenix. I'll be back in Seattle in a few days."

"Can you describe your vehicle?"

Pratt gave a description of his green Kenworth truck. The officer took down the information and ended the call. Within minutes, a teletype was sent to law enforcement agencies across the western states: Locate and arrest Jesse Pratt in connection with the murder of Carrie Love.

Later that same day, June 19, the Arizona Highway Patrol spotted a green Kenworth matching the description on a highway outside Phoenix. They pulled the truck over, and Jesse Pratt was taken into custody without incident.

Pratt was fifty-two years old, a large man with a matted beard and substantial belly. When questioned by Arizona authorities, his story began immediately.

"Carrie was with me, yes," he said. "We left Seattle together on the sixteenth, but she changed her mind about the trip. I dropped her off near the Seattle airport. She said she was going to fly home."

The investigators exchanged glances. Carrie's belongings had been found in Oregon, hundreds of miles from Seattle. Her body had been discovered even farther south.

Back in Oregon, the investigation was gathering momentum. Pratt's truck had been seized and was being processed by forensic technicians. What they found began to tell a very different story from the one Pratt was spinning.

Inside the truck's sleeping compartment, investigators discovered two rolls of Bounty paper towels, one opened. The towels were green—the same color as fragments found near Carrie's body. However, it was a detail noticed by forensic scientist Mike Howard that would prove significant. The paper towels from the crime scene had distinctive puncture marks along one edge, tiny holes created by wear on the manufacturing rollers during production. Howard compared them to the roll from Pratt's truck. The patterns matched exactly.

They found something else in the sleeping area—tiny fibers that matched those from the bloodstained sleeping bag discovered on the highway. The sleeping bag had been in Pratt's truck.

Meanwhile, Pratt's story was evolving. Confronted with evidence that Carrie had been in Oregon, he changed his account.

"Okay, she was with me the whole way," he admitted. "We had consensual sex at a truck stop. But then she told me she'd stolen six hundred dollars from the fuel money. I got angry and told her to get the hell out of my truck. I threw her stuff out and left her on the side of the road. There was a blue Scout there—I figured the driver would help her."

Investigators noted the detail about the blue Scout. Bruce McDonald had mentioned seeing such a vehicle near where the sleeping bag was found. Was Pratt incorporating real details into his fabricated story?

But it was the tire evidence that would prove most damning. The medical examiner had preserved the tire marks on Carrie's body—distinctive patterns pressed into her skin. Pete McDonald, a tire expert and former Firestone director of tire design, was brought in to analyze them.

McDonald studied the patterns on Carrie's arms and the strange burn mark on her left forearm. He examined Pratt's truck, making plaster casts of all the tires. The right rear tire had been retreaded two months before the murder, creating a unique pattern where the retread had been spliced together. McDonald traced the serial number—XZA9219— back to the retreading company.

Their records showed the work had been completed in April 1986. The payment check had been signed by Carrie Love herself, in her role as Pratt's employee.

McDonald conducted a dramatic demonstration. He coated the plaster cast of the tire with red dye and rolled it across his own arm. The pattern it left was identical to the marks on

Carrie's body. The shortened bar at the splice point, the geometric pattern, even the burn mark from the tire's sidewall—everything matched perfectly.

There was another clue. Carrie had scratched at her attacker with such force that red cotton fibers were trapped beneath her fingernails. When Pratt was picked up, he happened to be wearing a red T-shirt, and microscopic testing tied those fibers directly to his clothing.

Among Pratt's business papers, they found a receipt for diesel fuel from Redd's Gas Station, dated June 17—the day Carrie's belongings were found. An employee at the station remembered him clearly.

"Big guy with a full beard and a pot belly," the witness said. "He was with a young, pretty girl. She looked nervous."

As the case against Pratt solidified, investigators began looking into his background. What they found was a history of violence that stretched back years.

In 1980, Pratt had been involved in a kidnapping case that bore disturbing similarities to Carrie's murder. He and an accomplice named David Whaley had abducted Pratt's ex-girlfriend, Teresa Lewis, from her workplace in Seattle. They'd bound and gagged her coworkers with duct tape—the same materials used on Carrie. They'd then driven Teresa to Oregon—the same state where Carrie was killed. At a motel near Eugene, Pratt had forced Teresa to have sex with both men.

Teresa had managed to escape the next morning by slipping a business card to a woman with a plea to call for help. Pratt had been arrested and convicted of kidnapping, receiving a ten-year sentence. However, he'd only served thirty-nine months—less than half his term—before being released in 1984.

A prison psychologist had warned authorities at the time of his release: "Whoever releases this man must bear responsibility for his actions."

Now, two years after that early release, a young woman was dead.

The investigators also discovered that Pratt lived in the same Skyway apartment complex where another young woman, Virginia Rambus, had disappeared in May 1985. Virginia, just nineteen years old, had vanished while walking to a coworker's apartment. She'd never been found. Pratt was known in that neighborhood as the "Candy Man"—someone who provided drugs to local teenagers. He'd had access to a yellow 1978 Cadillac Eldorado at the time, similar to a vehicle seen in the area when Virginia had disappeared.

———

The trial began in January 1988 at the Klamath County Courthouse. Pratt was charged with two counts of aggravated murder—killing Carrie Love in the course of attempted rape, and killing her in the course of intentionally maiming her.

The prosecution laid out its case methodically. Pete McDonald took the stand and demonstrated his tire analysis, rolling the dyed plaster cast across his own arm in front of the jury. The red marks it left were identical to those photographed on Carrie's body.

"The tire that made these marks," McDonald testified, "was retreaded exactly two months before Miss Love's death. The serial number traces back to Pratt's truck. The check for the work was signed by the victim herself."

Mike Howard explained the paper towel evidence, showing how the distinctive puncture marks on towels from the crime scene matched those in Pratt's truck exactly.

Multiple witnesses testified that Pratt had later admitted to killing Carrie. He'd told several people about it, unable to keep the crime to himself.

Pratt took the stand in his own defense, an odd figure with his unkempt appearance and rambling explanations. He stuck to his story about abandoning Carrie by the roadside after an argument over money.

"I didn't hurt her," he insisted. "Someone else must have killed her. Maybe it was whoever was in that blue Scout."

But the evidence was overwhelming. The jury found Jesse Pratt guilty on both counts of aggravated murder. On February 22, 1988, he was sentenced to death by lethal injection.

Sadly, the conviction wouldn't stand. In 1990, the Oregon Supreme Court overturned it, ruling that evidence of Pratt's 1980 kidnapping had been improperly admitted during the guilt phase of the trial. The appeals court found that while both crimes involved taking women from Washington to Oregon, the differences were too significant—the 1980 crime involved a public abduction with an accomplice but no murder, while Carrie's case involved no accomplice but ended in brutal murder.

Pratt was retried in 1991. This time, prosecutors focused solely on the forensic evidence and witness testimony about Carrie's murder. Once again, the jury convicted him on both counts. Once again, he was sentenced to death.

This conviction was upheld by the Oregon Supreme Court in 1993. Pratt's appeals continued for years, with his attorneys raising claims about inadequate counsel and mental capacity. Psychological evaluations revealed that Pratt had an IQ of 77, borderline intellectual functioning. Dr. Faulder Colby, a neuropsychologist, found evidence of organic brain damage affecting Pratt's ability to control his behavior. Dr. Ralph Underwager testified that Pratt had suffered extensive childhood sexual abuse, leading to his violent and dysfunctional relationships with women.

In 2009, following the U.S. Supreme Court's decision in Atkins v. Virginia—which prohibited executing individuals with intellectual disabilities—Pratt's sentence was commuted to life without parole. At seventy-four years old, after eighteen years on death row, he was moved to the general prison population.

Virginia Rambus has never been found. The nineteen-year-old's disappearance from the Skyway apartment complex in May 1985 remains unsolved. King County detectives continue to investigate whether Jesse Pratt was involved. The proximity, the timing—less than a year after his early release from prison—and his presence in the neighborhood all raise questions that may never be answered.

In 2012, detectives released photos of Pratt and the yellow Cadillac he'd had access to, hoping to generate new leads. They emphasized that he wasn't officially a suspect, just a person of interest they wanted to eliminate or confirm, but no breakthrough came.

For the families involved, the what-ifs haunted them. What if Pratt had served his full sentence for the 1980 kidnapping? He wouldn't have been free in 1985, when Virginia had disappeared. He wouldn't have been free in 1986 to kill Carrie Love. The prison psychologist's warning echoed through the years: whoever released this man must bear responsibility for his actions.

As of 2025, Jesse Pratt remains in Oregon State Penitentiary, serving life without parole. At ninety-one years old, he's one of the oldest inmates in the system. He'll die behind prison walls, never again able to harm another young woman. For Carrie Love's family, for Teresa Lewis, who survived, and perhaps for Virginia Rambus, whose fate remains unknown, it's the only resolution the system could ultimately provide—ensuring that Jesse Pratt's path of destruction finally, permanently ended.

CHAPTER 11
THEY'LL BLAME US

Patty Espinoza had been settling in for the evening in her Chula Vista apartment when she heard it—a woman's voice, high and panicked, cutting through the thin walls of the complex at 1430 Hilltop Drive. In the two years she'd lived there, Patty had heard plenty through those walls. Arguments, laughter, the occasional party…but this was different. This was the sound of genuine terror.

She stepped outside to investigate and found her neighbor, Veronica Gonzales, in the hallway. The twenty-eight-year-old woman's face was streaked with tears, her hands shaking as she gestured frantically toward her apartment.

"My niece," Veronica gasped. "She's been burned in the bathtub. Please, you have to help."

It was July 21, 1995, a typical Friday evening in Southern California, still warm even as night fell. Patty started toward the apartment, but Veronica grabbed her arm. "Don't call the police," she said, her grip surprisingly firm. "Please, just don't call the police."

The request struck Patty as odd—why wouldn't someone want emergency services for an injured child?—but she followed Veronica inside. The apartment smelled of stale food and something else, something chemical and sharp. Toys were scattered across the floor, and children's voices came from behind a closed door. What Patty saw in the middle of that small, cluttered living room would haunt her for the rest of her life.

A small body lay on the floor. Four-year-old Genny Rojas was naked, her lower body covered in what looked like severe burns. The skin from her waist to her feet appeared raw and damaged, peeling away in places, and she wasn't moving.

"I need to get my sister," Patty said, her mind racing. "Noemi knows CPR."

While Patty ran to get her sister, Veronica's husband, Ivan Gonzales, appeared in the doorway. The thirty-one-year-old man seemed strangely calm, almost detached, as he looked down at the child's body. When Noemi Espinoza, a trained nurse's assistant, arrived moments later, Ivan picked up Genny and carried her across the hall to the Espinozas' apartment.

Noemi immediately began checking for vital signs. The child's body was cold to the touch, already showing signs of rigor mortis. Her skin and the t-shirt she wore were completely dry, which seemed inconsistent with Veronica's claim that she'd just pulled the girl from a bathtub. As Noemi attempted CPR, she noticed other disturbing details: a large bald spot on the child's head where the scalp appeared scarred, marks on her neck and arms, and bruising on her legs.

"Don't call the police because they will blame us for it!" Veronica suddenly cried out, confirming what Noemi had already begun to suspect—this was no accident.

Despite Veronica's protests, Noemi's husband had already dialed 911. The call was logged at 9:20 p.m.

Sergeant Barry Bennett of the Chula Vista Police Department arrived at the scene within minutes. A veteran officer with years of experience, Bennett had responded to countless emergency calls, but something about this one immediately set off his instincts.

He found the child lying on the carpet in the Espinoza apartment, surrounded by concerned neighbors. Bennett knelt beside the small body and performed his own check for vital signs. Nothing. The child was cold, rigid, and had clearly been dead for some time—far longer than the few minutes Veronica claimed had passed since discovering her in the tub.

Bennett noticed the extensive burns covering the lower portion of the child's body, from approximately the waist down, but it was the pattern of the burns that caught his attention. There were "spared areas"—patches of unburned skin behind the knees, in parts of the groin, and on the buttocks. This wasn't consistent with a child accidentally scalding herself in a bathtub. This pattern suggested the child had been held in a specific position, possibly forced into a fetal position, while the burning occurred.

While Bennett secured the scene, Veronica approached him with an explanation. She said she'd been cooking dinner when she'd put Genny in the bathtub. She'd started the water and left the child alone for about twenty minutes. When she returned, she claimed she found Genny face-down in the water, badly burned. The child must have turned on the hot water herself, Veronica suggested, not knowing how to adjust the temperature.

The story didn't add up. Bennett observed that, despite Veronica's claim of just pulling the child from the water, both Genny's hair and skin were completely dry. If she'd been submerged in water just minutes ago, there should have been some moisture.

Ivan sat nearby during this conversation, and Bennett noted his demeanor—eerily calm, almost nonchalant, given that his niece lay dead just feet away. When asked for his version of events, Ivan largely echoed his wife's story but added that Genny had a habit of "peeling and picking at her own skin," which he claimed explained some of the marks on her body.

Bennett called for homicide detectives and the medical examiner. This was clearly no accidental drowning.

———

As investigators began processing the scene, they started with the Gonzales apartment. The two-bedroom unit was cramped and cluttered, home to Ivan, Veronica, and their six biological children: eight-year-old Ivan Jr., seven-year-old Michael, six-year-old Vanessa, three-year-old Anthony, two-year-old Valerie, and one-month-old Alex. Nine people in total had been living in this small space.

Ivan and Veronica Gonzales

The bathroom told an interesting story. When detectives examined it shortly after the incident, they found the bathtub completely dry. The bathroom floor was dry as well. If a child had been pulled from a full tub of water just an hour earlier, there should have been some evidence of water—splashes on the floor, dampness on the tub walls, something. Instead, the bathroom looked like it hadn't been used in hours.

But then, investigators made a crucial discovery. In the bathtub drain and stuck to the tub itself, they found small pieces of human tissue. Lab tests would later confirm this tissue was consistent with Genny's DNA. So she had been in the tub, and she had been burned there. However, the timeline and circumstances were clearly different from what the Gonzales couple claimed.

Detectives conducted a test of the apartment's water system. They plugged the drain and turned on only the hot water tap. It took approximately fifteen minutes to fill the tub to about 8.5 inches deep, with the water reaching approximately 140 degrees Fahrenheit. At that temperature, forensic experts would later determine, it would take only six to ten seconds of immersion to cause the kind of deep burns found on Genny's body.

This wasn't a case of a child accidentally turning on water that was too hot. Someone had deliberately spent fifteen minutes filling the tub with scalding water—a calculated preparation that showed clear premeditation. Then, they had forced the child into that water and held her there for those crucial seconds, long enough to inflict fatal burns.

―――――

As investigators moved through the apartment, it was what they found in the master bedroom that would reveal the true horror of Genny's life in that apartment.

In the bedroom closet, they discovered something that made investigators pause. The closet doors were off their sliding tracks, leaning inward. One door had a hole cut into it, positioned at about eye level for an adult, perfect for observing whatever was inside. The smell hit them first—a mixture of blood, feces, and something else, something that spoke of prolonged suffering.

When detectives looked closer, they found a metal hook that had been fastened to the closet's hanger bar bracket, reinforced with cloth to bear weight. Directly below the hook, on the closet floor, sat a small wooden box, roughly two feet in all dimensions.

The walls told a horrifying story. Blood stains covered various surfaces—the back wall at different heights, the hook itself, the wooden box, and the interior of the closet door. Some stains showed the pattern of hair being wiped or dragged against the wall. Others were splatter patterns consistent with a bleeding person swinging or flailing. In some areas, investigators found what appeared to be bloody handprints and footprints, small ones, child-sized, as if someone had been trying to brace themselves against the walls.

Inside the wooden box, the forensic team found more blood stains along with fecal matter. The implications were sickening—a child had been kept in this box, possibly for extended periods, unable to leave even to use the bathroom.

Crime lab technicians carefully collected samples from throughout the closet. DNA testing would later confirm what investigators already suspected: the blood belonged to Genny Rojas.

In the same bedroom, behind the door, investigators found a piece of string tied from the doorknob to a nightstand—a makeshift restraint system that would have trapped anyone trying to open the door from that side, effectively imprisoning someone in the small space behind it. Near this area, about thirty-six inches off the floor—roughly the height of a four-year-old child's head—they discovered a dent in the drywall with blood spatter in and around it. The blood matched Genny's DNA.

As the evidence mounted, investigators also recovered several items that would prove significant: a hair dryer with a distinctive grill pattern on its front, a pair of small handcuffs, and various cords and cloth strips that appeared to have been used as restraints.

The San Diego County Medical Examiner performed the autopsy on Genny Rojas the morning after her death. What was found painted a picture of prolonged, systematic torture that had likely lasted months.

The immediate cause of death was clear: thermal burns covering the lower portion of her body, from waist to feet. These were second- to third-degree burns, so severe that skin had peeled away in many areas. The burn pattern, with those distinctive spared areas behind the knees and buttocks, confirmed that Genny had been held in a forced fetal position while immersed in scalding water. She would have died within two to three hours of suffering these burns, going into shock and organ failure without medical treatment.

But the fatal burns were just the final chapter in a much longer story of abuse.

The child's head showed multiple injuries. A large, partially healed burn covered the top of her scalp, extending to the back of her head and neck. This burn was at least a week old, infected, and had caused permanent hair loss in that area. The pattern suggested hot liquid had been poured over her head from above.

Her face bore distinctive grid-pattern burns on both cheeks that matched exactly with the hair dryer found in the apartment. Similar burns appeared on her shoulders and left upper arm. These were fresh injuries, likely inflicted within a day or two of death.

The autopsy revealed bruising around both eyes, inflicted within the last forty-eight hours of her life. Her lower lip was lacerated and torn away from the gum, consistent with a powerful blow to the mouth. Multiple small cuts and abrasions on her face matched the pattern of being struck with a hairbrush.

Most disturbingly, the medical examiner found evidence of repeated strangulation. A healing ligature mark on her neck extended behind her left ear, approximately one to two weeks old. Another scar ran from her jawbone to under her chin. Pinpoint hemorrhages in her right eye were classic signs of asphyxiation.

Genny's brain showed two separate injuries: a recent subdural hematoma (bleeding inside the skull) from within the last day of her life, likely from a violent blow or shaking, and an older brain hemorrhage from weeks or months earlier.

Her arms bore parallel scars that matched perfectly with the handcuffs found in the apartment. Additional abrasions on her wrists and arms were consistent with being bound with rope or cloth. Her heels showed ulcerated areas near the Achilles tendons, suggesting her ankles had been bound for extended periods.

Perhaps most telling of the chronic nature of the abuse was the condition of Genny's thymus gland. The medical examiner found it severely atrophied—shrunken far below normal size. The thymus, a small organ in the chest that helps develop the immune system in children, shrinks dramatically under conditions of extreme, prolonged stress—a physiological marker seen almost exclusively in victims of chronic abuse.

The medical examiner's conclusion was unequivocal: Genny Rojas had been systematically tortured over a period of months before her death.

The morning after Genny's death, detectives faced a delicate task. They needed to interview the six Gonzales children, who might be the only witnesses to what had really happened in that apartment.

Eight-year-old Ivan Jr. initially told investigators a story that mirrored his parents' account. Genny, his cousin, had been in the bathtub, he said, and had accidentally burned herself. His younger siblings either claimed to know nothing or repeated similar versions of an accidental death.

But something about Ivan Jr.'s demeanor troubled the detective conducting the interview. The boy seemed nervous, his small hands gripping the edge of the table. He kept glancing toward the door, his whole body tense, as if expecting his parents to walk in at any moment. His voice was barely above a whisper, and he seemed to be reciting words he'd memorized rather than describing what he'd actually seen.

When the detective gently urged him to "be more truthful," the child's composure began to crack. His eyes filled with tears, and his hands started shaking. For several long moments, he said nothing at all. Then, in a rush, as if the words had been trapped inside him, the real story began to pour out.

He admitted that he and his siblings had been locked in their bedroom when Genny died. Their bedroom door had no doorknob; it had a slide-lock on the outside, which their parents used to keep them confined, but Ivan Jr. had watched through the hole where the doorknob should have been.

What he described was far different from the accident his parents claimed.

Ivan Jr. had seen his parents put Genny in the bathtub many times before. They would run hot water over her while she screamed. On multiple occasions, he'd watched his father hold Genny's head down while his mother poured hot water, both actively participating. This wasn't something that happened once—it was a repeated form of punishment.

The boy's testimony grew more disturbing as he continued. He'd seen Genny hanging in the closet, sometimes in the box, sometimes suspended with her feet off the ground. He'd watched both parents pull out Genny's hair with their hands. He'd seen them tie her up and leave her bound for hours.

When Genny first came to live with them five months earlier, Ivan Jr. said, "She had all her hair and no marks or bruises." Everything had happened after she arrived.

The children had been forced to participate in the abuse in small ways. Their parents made them throw balls at Genny as a form of torment. Ivan Jr. said he would deliberately aim to miss because he didn't want to hurt his cousin.

Six-year-old Vanessa later confirmed her brother's account about the food. She whispered to investigators that she would try to sneak crackers to Genny when their parents weren't looking. "Genny was so hungry," she said. "She would cry. But if Mommy caught us, we got hit with the belt."

As for the story about Genny accidentally tipping over a pot of boiling water on herself (the explanation for her head burns), Ivan Jr. was clear: He'd never seen any such accident. What he had seen was his parents deliberately burning her with hot water, over and over again.

As investigators dug deeper into the case, they began to piece together Genny's tragic journey to the Gonzales home.

The little girl's life had been marked by instability from the beginning. Her mother, Mary Rojas, struggled with drug addiction. Her father, Pete Rojas, was in prison for child molestation—he'd pleaded guilty to sexually abusing Genny's older half-sister. In April 1994, when Genny was just three years old, she and her siblings had been removed from their parents' custody.

The children went first to their maternal grandmother, Utilia Ortiz, then to other relatives. By February 1995, after being passed between family members who found her difficult to manage, Genny ended up with Veronica and Ivan Gonzales. It was meant to be temporary, with a promise of financial help that never came.

The Gonzales family was already under severe strain. Their welfare benefits were running out, utilities were frequently shut off, and they often went without food. Despite these hardships, both Ivan and Veronica were spending what money they had on methamphetamine.

This informal family arrangement had a critical flaw: no social worker supervision. San Diego County's child protection services had no knowledge of Genny's placement with the Gonzales family. There would be no check-ins, no visits, no oversight. For five months, Genny would be invisible to the system that was supposed to protect her.

―――

The timeline of Genny's final hours began to come together through witness statements and evidence.

Around 8:45 p.m., neighbors heard a loud bang or thud from the Gonzales apartment, immediately followed by the sound of a child crying. The crying stopped abruptly. A neighbor saw Ivan come to the window, look out with an angry expression, and forcefully shut it. He then stormed out of the apartment, slamming the door behind him.

Ivan walked to a nearby liquor store where he was a regular customer, arriving at around 8:45 or 8:50 p.m. He purchased milk, cereal, and candy on credit, appearing to be in a hurry. He returned to the apartment complex by approximately 8:55 p.m.

What happened in those ten minutes while Ivan was gone? Based on the medical evidence and the condition of Genny's body when help was finally called, investigators believed this was when the fatal scalding occurred. The loud bang neighbors heard was likely Genny being forced into the scalding water or struggling against it.

When Ivan returned, neither he nor Veronica sought help for the dying child. Instead, they waited. For at least an hour, possibly longer, they left Genny to succumb to her injuries. The medical examiner determined that with prompt medical attention, she would have had a 90 percent chance of survival. As the minutes ticked by and she went into shock, her organs began to fail from the massive trauma of the burns.

It wasn't until after 9:00 p.m.—when Genny was likely already dead or very close to death—that Veronica began screaming for help. Even then, her primary concern seemed to be avoiding police involvement. Her repeated pleas to neighbors not to call authorities, her statement that "they will blame us for it," suggested she knew exactly how damaging the evidence would be.

By the time paramedics arrived at 9:25 p.m., Genny had been dead long enough for rigor mortis to set in. Emergency crews attempted to prepare the child for CPR but found her jaw clenched shut—another sign of rigor mortis. Her body was cool, with no pulse and no chance of revival.

———

In the early morning hours of July 22, 1995, both Ivan and Veronica Gonzales were arrested and charged with murder. Both tested positive for methamphetamine.

At 9:45 that morning, Ivan was interviewed by detectives. He stuck to the story that Genny's death was accidental, that she must have turned on water that was too hot while unsupervised. When confronted with the evidence of older injuries, he had explanations for everything. He claimed the burn on her head came from when she knocked over a pot of boiling water weeks earlier. The ligature mark on her neck was supposedly from neighbor kids pulling on a candy necklace. As for the grid-pattern burns on her face that matched the hair dryer, he insisted he hadn't even noticed them.

When asked about the closet with its hook and box, Ivan's story shifted slightly. Yes, he admitted, they had made Genny sleep in the closet "a few times." They'd put her in the box "a couple of times to scare her." But the hook? That was just meant to frighten her—he insisted he'd never actually tied her to it. The handcuffs found in the apartment? They'd never used those on Genny, though he did concede that Veronica had "tied her hands with a cloth once."

Veronica's initial interview followed a similar pattern of denial and minimization. However, as detectives presented her with evidence and witness statements, cracks began to appear in her story. When she learned that Ivan was also being questioned and might be blaming her, her narrative started to shift. She began to portray herself as another victim, dominated and abused by her husband, unable to protect Genny from his violence.

The trials of Ivan and Veronica Gonzales would reveal the full extent of Genny's suffering and the dynamics of the household where she died. Prosecutors presented a case of systematic torture lasting approximately six months. The physical evidence was overwhelming: the burns, the ligature marks, the handcuff scars, the blood-stained closet, the DNA evidence.

But it was the testimony of Ivan Jr., delivered via videotape to spare him from facing his parents in court, that provided the most damning account of what life was like for Genny in that apartment.

Both defendants attempted to shift blame to the other. Ivan's defense portrayed him as a passive, submissive husband dominated by an aggressive wife. Veronica's defense claimed she suffered from battered woman syndrome, arguing that years of abuse from Ivan had rendered her psychologically unable to protect Genny.

The prosecution countered both narratives with evidence that both parents had actively participated in the torture. The forensic evidence suggested that holding a struggling child in scalding water would require two people. Multiple witnesses, including the children, had seen both parents committing acts of abuse.

In November 1997, Ivan Gonzales was found guilty of first-degree murder with special circumstances of torture. When the jury couldn't reach a unanimous verdict on sentencing, a second jury was empaneled for the penalty phase. In January 1998, he was sentenced to death.

Veronica's trial came months later. In May 1998, she, too, was found guilty of first-degree murder with special circumstances of torture and mayhem. The jury again recommended death. On July 20, 1998, Judge Michael Wellington formally imposed the death sentence.

In his statement at sentencing, Judge Wellington called it the most heinous case of child abuse he'd encountered in twenty-six years as a lawyer and judge. Ivan and Veronica Gonzales became the first married couple in California history to receive death sentences for the same crime.

The murder of Genny Rojas exposed critical gaps in the child welfare system. The informal arrangement that placed her with the Gonzales family had occurred entirely outside official channels. No social worker had supervised the placement. No one had checked on Genny's welfare during the five months she lived in that apartment.

The California Supreme Court would later uphold both death sentences—Veronica's in 2011, Ivan's in 2012. The court found that the evidence of prolonged torture was "overwhelming," and the facts were "almost unimaginably horrible."

Both Ivan and Veronica Gonzales remain on California's death row today, their executions indefinitely postponed by the state's moratorium on capital punishment. They are serving what amounts to life sentences, separated in different prisons.

CHAPTER 12
THE CLEVELAND MONSTER

Michelle Knight stood at the corner of West 106th Street and Lorain Avenue, squinting at the crumpled paper in her hand. August 23, 2002. The custody hearing was in less than an hour, and she couldn't find the damn building.

At twenty-one, Michelle looked younger—under five feet tall, barely a hundred pounds. People often mistook her for a teenager. Today, that didn't matter. What mattered was getting to the courthouse, convincing the judge she could take care of Joey again. Her two-year-old son. She'd lost custody after an accident that wasn't really her fault, but try explaining that to social services.

The maroon van that pulled up alongside her seemed like salvation.

She recognized the driver immediately. It was the father of someone she knew from the neighborhood—she'd been to his daughter Arlene's house before. Ariel Castro. That was his name. Forty-two years old, thick dark hair, a mustache. He worked as a school bus driver and played bass guitar in

Latin bands around Cleveland. Arlene lived with her mother now, and she had for years.

"You look lost, mija."

Michelle explained about the social services building and the custody hearing. Castro nodded knowingly. Of course he knew where it was—he drove all over the city for work. But first, he needed to stop at his house real quick. Just a minute. Plus, he mentioned, his dog just had puppies. She could pick one out for her son. Wouldn't Joey love that?

The house at 2207 Seymour Avenue looked ordinary. White siding, two stories, small front porch. Some trash in the yard, a few boarded windows, but nothing unusual for this part of Cleveland. Michelle followed Castro through the front door, expecting to hear puppies yipping somewhere in the back. Instead, she heard the deadbolt thud behind her.

Castro's expression changed so completely that it was like watching a mask slip off. The helpful neighbor was gone. In his place stood someone she'd never seen before.

"You're not going anywhere for a long time."

Before she could process the words, before she could scream, he had her on the ground. Orange extension cords wrapped around her wrists, her ankles, then her neck. She had one photo of Joey in her pocket, a Polaroid from his second birthday. Castro found it, held it up to the light, and then slowly tore it into pieces while she watched.

Ariel Castro

The basement was unfinished concrete, cold even in August. A single bare bulb hung from the ceiling, controlled by a switch upstairs. In the center of the room, a support pole ran from floor to ceiling. Castro had prepared for this—there were already chains attached to it.

The search for Michelle Knight lasted exactly fifteen months.

Police classified her as a voluntary missing person almost immediately. Adult woman, custody problems, history of family issues. The assumption was obvious: She'd run away, unable to face losing her son. Her mother and cousins searched on their own, putting up flyers and calling hospitals, but without media attention or police resources, they were just voices in the wind.

In November 2003, the FBI removed Michelle Knight from their missing persons database.

By then, she'd been in Castro's basement for over a year. The routine was established. Fed once a day, if she was lucky—chips, crackers, occasional McDonald's. The bucket he'd given her for a toilet was emptied maybe once a week. The stench made her retch, but retching when you're chained by the neck is its own special hell.

Castro would come down at night after his shifts driving the school bus. Sometimes he'd leave her chained in stress positions—arms above her head, legs spread, neck stretched just enough that she had to stay on her tiptoes or choke. He'd return days later to find her still there, muscles screaming, covered in her own waste.

The rapes were diabolical. He made her wear a motorcycle helmet during them, stifling her screams. Not that anyone would hear—he blared loud music to muffle any sound.

Winter in that basement nearly killed her. No heat reached the concrete room. Castro gave her a single blanket that reeked of motor oil. She learned to curl into the smallest possible ball, preserving what little body heat she had. Her periods stopped—malnutrition, stress, cold. A small mercy in hell.

―――

Spring came slowly to Cleveland in 2003. On April 21, the day before her seventeenth birthday, Amanda Berry finished her shift at Burger King on West 110th Street and called her sister.

"I'm getting a ride home," she said around 8:00 p.m.

Amanda knew the man who'd offered—Ariel Castro, whose daughter, Arlene, went to her school. She'd been to their house before for parties. He seemed safe enough, a familiar face in a familiar van.

Castro suggested stopping at his house first. Arlene was there, he said. They could say hi real quick.

But Arlene wasn't there.

Once inside 2207 Seymour Avenue, Amanda found herself shoved into a darkness she couldn't comprehend. Castro showed her around the house first—a sick kind of tour. He even led her to a back bedroom where a small woman lay motionless on a dirty mattress.

It was Michelle, drugged into unconsciousness.

Then came the basement. The chains. The realization that the stories you heard about, the warnings your mother gave you—they were all real, and they were happening right now.

The next day, Castro used Amanda's cell phone to call her mother, Louwana Miller.

"I have Amanda," he said. "She's fine and will be coming home in a couple of days."

Then he hung up and destroyed the phone.

The search for Amanda Berry was everything Michelle Knight's hadn't been. Media coverage, FBI involvement, family on television pleading for her return. Louwana Miller was relentless—appearing on "America's Most Wanted," organizing searches, and keeping her daughter's face in the public eye.

Inside the house, Castro had modified his prison to accommodate two captives. He moved them between the basement and upstairs bedrooms according to his paranoid whims. The windows throughout the house were covered first with heavy plastic, then boarded from the inside with thick plywood. He installed padlocks on every door—sometimes three or four on a single room. Motion detectors and makeshift alarms made from Radio Shack components were rigged to alert him if anyone tried to move without permission.

The psychological torture was precise. He would force Michelle and Amanda to watch news coverage of their own disappearances. There was Louwana on TV, crying, begging for information. There were the yellow ribbons, the candlelight vigils, the age-progressed photos showing what Amanda might look like now.

"See?" Castro would say to Michelle. "Nobody's looking for you. But her—they care about her."

He played games with them. Sometimes he'd leave a door unlocked, pretending to forget. If they tried to open it—even just tested the handle—alarms would shriek and the beatings would last hours. He was conditioning them like lab animals, teaching them that hope equaled pain.

Michelle became pregnant that first year. Castro's response was swift and brutal. He starved her for two weeks, allowing only sips of tea. He punched her stomach repeatedly with a barbell from his weight set. When that didn't work, he threw her down the basement stairs. The miscarriage came with so much blood that she thought she was dying.

It would happen four more times over the years. Each pregnancy ended the same way—starvation, beatings, forced exercises until her body gave up. The physical damage accumulated: hearing loss in one ear, facial fractures that never healed properly, and internal scarring that would leave her unable to have children even if she escaped.

A year passed. Two. The outside world moved on, as it always does.

On April 2, 2004, Gina DeJesus stood at a payphone on West 105th Street and Lorain Avenue. Fourteen years old, seventh grade, best friends with Arlene Castro. She'd just called her mother to ask if she could sleep over at Arlene's house.

"No, you come home."

Gina hung up, disappointed, and started walking. When Arlene's father pulled up in his maroon van, it seemed perfectly natural. She'd known him for years.

"You seen Arlene?" Castro asked through the window. "I'm looking for her."

Gina hadn't seen her, but she offered to help look. At the house, Castro asked her to help carry a stereo speaker inside. Teenage politeness—always help adults with heavy things.

The door closed. The lock clicked.

"That's the wrong door," Castro said when Gina turned toward what looked like an exit. "Let me show you the right way."

He led her down to the basement.

Three women now. Castro's house of horrors was complete.

He kept Gina and Michelle together in an upstairs bedroom, seven feet by eleven feet. Both chained to the same wall, they could reach each other but not the door. Amanda was isolated in another room—divide and conquer, basic psychology.

The room where Michelle and Gina were held had a small television that received three channels. They watched themselves become history. The vigils for Gina were massive—the Puerto Rican community in Cleveland rallied around the DeJesus family. Her mother, Nancy Ruiz, appeared on every show that would have her. The FBI released a composite sketch of a suspect that looked nothing like Castro.

Unbelievably, Castro attended those vigils. He stood with the community, holding candles, comforting Gina's mother. He helped distribute missing person flyers with Gina's face on them. His son, Anthony, a journalism student at Bowling Green State University, even wrote an article about the disappearances for the Plain Press, interviewing Nancy Ruiz about her missing daughter.

"She's still alive," Nancy told Anthony Castro. "I can feel it."

Anthony included the quote in his article, never knowing his father kept Gina chained in a bedroom three miles away.

November 2004 brought a devastating blow. Louwana Miller went on "The Montel Williams Show," where psychic Sylvia Browne told her that Amanda was dead, that she could see her "in water." Louwana took down the missing posters. She stopped the searches. Sixteen months later, she died of heart failure. She was forty-three years old.

Castro made Amanda watch the footage of her mother's funeral on the news.

The years blurred together in predictable horror. Wake up chained. Use the bucket. Eat the single meal—always McDonald's or Burger King, Castro's little joke. Submit to whatever he demanded. Sleep. Repeat.

They found ways to cope. When Castro gave them paper—rare treats—they kept diaries. The entries were evidence of minds fighting not to break:

"I want my freedom. I am tired of crying. I am tired of being alone. I am tired of being locked up. I am tired of being belittled. I am tired of being intimidated. I am tired of being abused."

They marked birthdays, holidays, anniversaries of their abductions. Time became their act of resistance.

In 2006, Amanda discovered she was pregnant. This time, Castro decided to let it happen. As Christmas approached, he prepared in his own twisted way. He brought a plastic kiddie pool to Amanda's room—the kind you'd fill with water for toddlers in the summer.

"You're going to deliver this baby," he told Michelle. "If it dies, I'll kill you."

December 25, 2006. No doctors, no medical supplies, just Michelle with her broken fingers and Amanda screaming through labor. The baby came out blue, not breathing. Michelle cleared the airways, breathed into the tiny lungs until a cry finally came. Amanda named her Jocelyn.

The child changed everything and nothing.

Castro doted on Jocelyn in his way. He brought her toys, clothes, and even took her outside sometimes—to the park, to visit his mother. He told people she was his girlfriend's daughter. His mother believed him, calling Jocelyn her granddaughter.

As the years passed, Jocelyn became the women's reason to survive. Amanda taught her to read using fast-food napkins and ketchup packets. They played school, pretending the locked bedroom was a classroom. The little girl called Castro "Daddy" because that's all she knew.

The outside world came close to discovering them several times. In January 2004, police visited the house after Castro left a child on his school bus. They knocked, got no answer, and left. In November 2011, neighbors called about pounding sounds from the house when Castro wasn't home. Police responded, knocked, walked around the property, found nothing suspicious, and left.

Two neighbors would later claim they saw naked women crawling in Castro's backyard on dog leashes. They said they called the police, but the police said they had no record of such calls.

Meanwhile, Castro's behavior grew more erratic. In November 2012, he was fired from his bus driver job for making an illegal U-turn with children aboard, using the bus for grocery shopping, and leaving a child unattended. Without the structure of work, he became unpredictable. Sometimes he was gone for days, leaving them chained without food. Sometimes he was home for weeks straight, watching them constantly.

He still played his sick games: Russian roulette, locked-door tests, and making them play "wife" for a day—cooking, cleaning, pretending to be a normal family while knowing that one wrong move meant days of starvation.

Monday, May 6, 2013, was a warm spring day in Cleveland. Ariel Castro left the house at around 5:30 p.m. to visit his brother. For the first time in eleven years, he forgot to lock the inner door properly. The heavy wooden door between the living room and enclosed porch stood unlocked. Only the storm door's bolt remained.

Amanda noticed. She'd been moved to a downstairs bedroom after Jocelyn was born, giving her more freedom of movement than the others. Hesitantly, she touched the doorknob. It turned.

This had to be a test. Another game. Touch the door, get beaten. Hope equals pain—he'd taught them that lesson thoroughly.

But Jocelyn had watched from the window. "Daddy's car is gone."

Amanda Berry made a choice. She pushed through to the enclosed porch, trapped now between the inner door and the bolted storm door. She could see the street through the glass. Normal people living normal lives, no idea what existed inside this house.

She began pounding on the storm door, managed to get her arm through a gap, screaming with a voice raw from years of forced silence.

"Help me! Please help me! I need help!"

Angel Cordero heard her first but couldn't understand her English. Then Charles Ramsey, walking home with his dinner, heard the screaming. He saw the arm waving frantically through the gap in the door.

"I've been here a long time," Amanda gasped. "I need help getting out!"

Ramsey kicked the bottom of the storm door repeatedly until the aluminum buckled. Amanda squeezed through the opening, clutching Jocelyn, her daughter who had never known freedom.

"Call 911! My name is Amanda Berry!"

Ramsey's face went white. He knew that name. Everyone in Cleveland knew that name.

———

The 911 call lasted just minutes, but it changed everything.

"I've been kidnapped, and I've been missing for ten years, and I'm here. I'm free now," Amanda told the dispatcher, her words tumbling over each other. "I'm at 2207 Seymour Avenue."

"Are there others in the house?"

"Yes. Gina DeJesus and another girl."

Officers Anthony Espada and Barbara Johnson arrived within minutes. Upstairs, they found Michelle and Gina still chained, unable to believe this was real. After so many tricks, so many tests, how could they trust that these were really the police?

Michelle launched herself at Officer Espada, sobbing, "You saved us! You saved us!"

Gina emerged more slowly, as if walking through a dream she didn't want to wake from.

While the women were being treated, Cleveland police searched for Ariel Castro. They found him at a McDonald's parking lot, sitting in his car. The arrest was surprisingly mundane—no resistance, no dramatic confrontation. He was taken into custody along with his brothers, Pedro and Onil, though the brothers would be released within days when it became clear that they had no knowledge of the crimes.

The search of the home revealed the full extent of Ariel's elaborate prison. Investigators found chains hanging from the ceiling, slots cut in doors for food delivery, the alarms he had rigged, and the thoroughly boarded windows. They also found the women's diaries, which would become crucial evidence.

In one particularly chilling discovery, investigators found a letter Ariel had written years earlier, apparently as a suicide note. In it, he had confessed to the kidnappings, calling himself a "sexual predator" and attempting to blame his behavior on his own childhood abuse. He had written about his victims by name, even leaving them money in his will—an admission of guilt written years before his capture.

The house also contained hundreds of feet of chain, multiple padlocks, and the motorcycle helmets he had forced the women to wear during assaults to muffle their screams. In the basement, investigators could see where the paint had been worn away from the support pole Michelle had been chained to for months, her desperate attempts to escape leaving physical marks on the structure itself.

As news of the rescue spread, Cleveland erupted in a mixture of celebration and horror. These women had been missing for years, their faces on posters throughout the city. Amanda and Gina's families had never stopped searching, holding vigils, appearing on television, maintaining hope against all odds. Now they were alive, found just miles from where they had disappeared.

The details that emerged in the following days stunned investigators. The systematic torture, the forced miscarriages, the birth of Jocelyn in captivity—each revelation was more horrifying than the last. The fact that Castro had participated in searches for his own victims, had comforted their families while holding their daughters prisoner, revealed a level of sadistic calculation that was difficult to comprehend.

For Michelle, the rescue was bittersweet. Unlike Amanda and Gina, she had no family waiting for her. Her disappearance had been largely ignored, her name removed from missing persons databases. The son she had been trying to regain custody of had been adopted by another family. After eleven years, she might have been free, but she faced the challenge of rebuilding a life from nothing.

The legal proceedings moved swiftly. Prosecutors initially charged Castro with four counts of kidnapping and three counts of rape. By July 12, the charges had expanded to 977 total counts: 512 counts of kidnapping, 446 counts of rape, 7 counts of gross sexual imposition, 6 counts of felonious assault, 3 counts of child endangerment, 2 counts of aggravated murder for the forced miscarriages, and 1 count of possession of criminal tools.

On July 26, 2013, faced with the possibility of the death penalty, Castro accepted a plea deal: guilty to 937 counts in exchange for life in prison without parole plus a thousand years. He also forfeited all assets, including the house, and waived his right to appeal.

At his sentencing hearing on August 1, 2013, the courtroom heard from the victims themselves. Michelle Knight confronted Castro directly: "I spent eleven years in hell. Now your hell is just beginning. I can forgive you, but I will never forget."

Castro delivered a rambling statement claiming:

"These people are trying to paint me as a monster. I'm not a monster. I'm sick... Most of the sex that went on in the house, and probably all of it, was consensual."

He blamed pornography addiction and claimed childhood sexual abuse.

Judge Michael Russo responded:

"There is no place in this city, there is no place in this country, there is no place in this world for those who enslave others. You will never be released from incarceration during the period of your remaining natural life for any reason."

———

The house on Seymour Avenue was demolished on August 7, 2013, with Michelle Knight present for the ceremony. She handed out yellow balloons to the crowd—symbols of missing children everywhere—and released them into the sky as the excavator took its first bite into the structure. Where a house of horrors had stood, there would be only an empty lot, and eventually, a memorial garden.

One month later, on September 3, 2013, guards found Ariel Castro hanging in his prison cell. He had fashioned a noose from bedsheets and hanged himself during the night. Some suggested it might have been auto-erotic asphyxiation gone wrong, but the official ruling was suicide. The monster who had controlled every aspect of three women's lives for a decade had chosen his own exit.

Amanda, Gina, and Michelle began the long process of healing. They wrote books, started foundations, and became advocates for missing persons. Amanda took a job with a local news station, helping to find other missing children. Gina co-founded the Cleveland Family Center for Missing Children and Adults. Michelle, who legally changed her name to Lily Rose Lee, wrote two memoirs and founded an animal rescue organization.

Ten years after their escape, they had built new lives from the ashes of their captivity. They had survived what few could imagine, emerging not as victims but as voices for those still missing, still hoping, still fighting to come home.

Online Appendix

Visit my website for additional photos and videos pertaining to the cases in this book:

http://TrueCrimeCaseHistories.com/vol21/

More books by Jason Neal

Looking for more?? I am constantly adding new volumes of True Crime Case Histories. The series **can be read in any order,** and all books are available in paperback, hardcover, and audiobook.

Check out the complete series on Amazon series at:

https://geni.us/JasonNeal

FREE BONUS EBOOK FOR MY READERS

As my way of saying "Thank you" for reading, I'm giving away a FREE True Crime e-book I think you'll enjoy.

https://TrueCrimeCaseHistories.com

Just visit the link above to let me know where to send your free book!

THANK YOU!

Thank you for reading this Volume of True Crime Case Histories. I truly hope you enjoyed it. If you did, I would be sincerely grateful if you would take a few minutes to write a review for me on Amazon using the link below.

https://geni.us/TrueCrime21

I'd also like to encourage you to sign up for my email list for updates, discounts, and freebies on future books! I promise I'll make it worth your while with future freebies.

http://truecrimecasehistories.com

And please take a moment and follow me on Amazon.

http://amazon.com/author/jason-neal/

Thanks so much,

Jason Neal

ABOUT THE AUTHOR

Jason Neal is a Best-Selling American True Crime Author living in Hawaii with his Turkish-British wife. Jason started his writing career in the late eighties as a music industry publisher and wrote his first true crime collection in 2019.

As a boy growing up in the eighties just south of Seattle, Jason became interested in true crime stories after hearing the news of the Green River Killer so close to his home. Over the subsequent years, he would read everything he could get his hands on about true crime and serial killers.

As he approached 50, Jason began to assemble stories of the crimes that have fascinated him most throughout his life. He's especially obsessed by cases solved by sheer luck, amazing police work, and groundbreaking technology like early DNA cases and, more recently, reverse genealogy.

Printed in Dunstable, United Kingdom